Japanese comfort food

ソウルフード

DK

Japanese comfort food

市原沙織

DELICIOUS EVERYDAY HOME COOKING

ソウルフード

Saori Ichihara

PHOTOGRAPHY BY YLVA SUNDGREN

Contents
もくじ

Introduction ———— 7

Pantry ———— 9
Noodles ———— 25
Rice ———— 45
Deep fried ———— 73
Fried & grilled ———— 95
Stews & soups ———— 117
Small plates ———— 131

A Japanese meal ———— 148

Index ———— 150

Introduction　　はじめに

I was born and grew up in Japan before moving to Sweden in 2014. One of the many ways I have coped with my homesickness has been to eat Japanese food in my new homeland, ideally using everyday ingredients that I can easily get from the nearest supermarket whenever I feel the craving. But I still always want to get the most authentic result I can, because when my stomach is full of the flavours of home, I feel strong again.

For me and my daughter, Myo, dinner at home is often based on Japanese flavours, and since I've become a mother, it's become more important for me to be able to cook quickly and easily at home, even during hectic weeks.

This book is for anyone curious about Japanese cuisine and who wants to bring those flavours into their everyday meals. Here, I've brought together the most popular comfort-food dishes we eat in Japan. The recipes are written to make it easy for you to succeed with them in your own kitchen, with helpful tips ensuring you avoid common pitfalls and mistakes, and ultimately boost your overall cooking technique.

Many recipes in the book are made with animal protein, but most of the sauces are vegan or vegetarian, so it's easy to make any of the dishes vegetarian by replacing the meat and fish with vegetables.

I've included useful basic sauces to also make it easier to include extra smaller dishes to your menu. Everyday logistics are much more straightforward if you make large batches of sauces. You can store them in the fridge and then it's easy to cook your choice of vegetables and protein and combine them with a sauce to make dinner prep a breeze.

Rice works well as an accompaniment to many of the dishes. My top tip here is to make a big batch of rice and freeze it in portions. Then, simply heat the rice in the microwave or in a steamer basket when it's time to eat.

I hope my book will inspire you to add more Japanese food to your weekly menu!

Saori Ichihara

Pantry

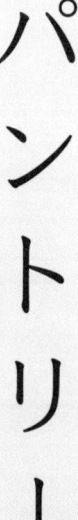

パントリー

Here is an overview of the flavours used in the book. I've kept it very simple, but it also gives you a picture of what my pantry of Japanese ingredients looks like in real life.

Many of these ingredients can be bought in supermarkets or in Asian shops, although genuine Japanese mirin with alcohol can be difficult to obtain in certain countries and you may need to order it online. However, the mirin you can buy in shops works perfectly well for the recipes in this book.

In this chapter I also share my very simple and delicious basic sauces that you can make and keep ready in the fridge. Hopefully, they will help make your everyday cooking less of a hassle!

Yuzu kosho

Panko

Coarse panko

Sesame oil

Aonori (seaweed powder)

Sesame seeds

Wasabi

Gari

Umeboshi

Mustard powder

Japanese (light) soy sauce

Round-grain (sticky) rice

Sesame paste

Useful basic sauces

Tare
SOY-BASED GLAZE

Tare is a soy-based glazing sauce. You can coat it on meat or fish, use it to fry in, or brush vegetables with it. It has a deep, rich flavour, which gives it that Japanese comfort-food feeling, and takes on an even more glorious scent when it's charred during frying or grilling. It smells so good! It's worth doubling the recipe if you want to make a larger batch, because it's so useful to have in the fridge.

MAKES ABOUT 300ML (1¼ CUPS)
90g (scant ½ cup) muscovado sugar
3½ tbsp rice vinegar
100ml (scant ½ cup) mirin
100ml (scant ½ cup) sake or dry white or red wine
200ml (scant 1 cup) Japanese soy sauce
5cm (2in) piece of kombu

PREPARATION
1. Bring the sugar and vinegar to the boil in a saucepan over a medium heat.
2. When the sugar mixture has taken on a syrupy consistency, add the mirin and sake (making sure they don't splash) and increase the heat, then reduce down to about half the volume.
3. Add the soy sauce and simmer for about 3 minutes, then add the kombu and leave to cool. Keeps for 1 month in the fridge.

TOP TIP! This is a delicious sauce that you can have with almost everything! Use it as a dip, a glaze, or a marinade. If you like, you can even choose to infuse the tare with spice (for example star anise, sansho pepper and/or chilli) in step 2.

Bannou sauce
ALL-ROUNDER SAUCE

A rich, heavy sauce consisting of many flavours blended together. This sauce was probably inspired by Western sauces from the time when a great deal of Western culture arrived in Japan. The sauce can be used for many of the dishes in the book, but sometimes needs to be adjusted slightly to suit the dish it will be served with.

MAKES ABOUT 300ML (1¼ CUPS)
4 tbsp miso paste
4 tbsp sugar
4 tbsp apple juice or grated apple
100g (scant ½ cup) ketchup
4 tbsp Japanese soy sauce
4 tbsp Worcestershire sauce

PREPARATION
1. Combine the miso with the sugar and apple juice in a mixing bowl, then add the remaining ingredients. Alternatively, place all the ingredients in a large bowl and mix with a hand-held blender. Keeps for 1 month in the fridge.

Taberu rayu
CHUNKY UMAMI OIL

Rayu originally comes from China, and is an oil infused with chilli for heat. It's often used to flavour sauces and stocks. This is a Japanese version that you can eat with rice or use as a sauce or topping. The oil is infused with chilli and other spices to bring out even more flavour. When cooked, all the water boils away, giving the oil a pleasant, crispy consistency.

MAKES ABOUT 400ML (1¾ CUPS)
4 garlic cloves, finely sliced
2 tbsp finely chopped ginger
50g (1¾oz) shiitake mushrooms, finely chopped
65g (2¼oz) onion, finely chopped
1 tbsp sesame seeds
3 tbsp crushed katsuobushi
30g (1oz) walnuts, cut into small pieces
1 tbsp Sichuan pepper, crushed
10 small whole dried chillies, crushed or sliced
⅓ tsp freshly ground black pepper
3½ tbsp light miso paste
2 tbsp sesame oil
300ml (1¼ cups) rapeseed (canola) oil

PREPARATION
1. Place all of the ingredients except the oils in a saucepan and mix thoroughly so the miso is evenly distributed. You can use one hand (wearing a kitchen glove to avoid getting chilli in your eyes later) to spread the miso through the mixture.
2. Pour in the oils and place over a high heat. When the mixture starts to bubble, reduce the heat to medium and continue stirring.
3. When it has almost stopped bubbling, turn off the heat and strain the oil into a mixing bowl. Cool the oil and solids separately, otherwise the hot oil will continue to cook the ingredients. Once everything is cool, mix it all together again and store in a jar. Keeps for 2 months in the fridge.

Ponzu
SOY & CITRUS

Ponzu is often sold in bottles and is usually made from soy sauce and various kinds of citrus such as yuzu, lemon, lime, or sudachi. In the ponzu section of food shops in Japan, there are a wide range of varieties, while in Sweden it's almost impossible to get hold of any. But it's incredibly easy to make it yourself! This way you can also adjust the acid and the combination of citrus fruits you use. This is my home recipe. I use muscovado sugar instead of mirin to achieve a deeper flavour. It's delicious simply drizzled over salad or silken tofu, or used to flavour fried or blanched vegetables!

MAKES ABOUT 200ML (SCANT 1 CUP)
100ml (scant ½ cup) Japanese soy sauce
3½ tbsp lemon juice (from about 1 large lemon)
3½ tbsp lime juice (from about 2–3 limes)
5cm (2in) piece of kombu
½ tbsp muscovado sugar
a few pieces of lemon and lime zest

PREPARATION
1. Place all of the ingredients in a saucepan and warm over a medium heat until the liquid starts to bubble a little at the edge of the pan. Turn off the heat and leave to cool, then strain. Keeps for 1 month in the fridge.

Gomadare

SESAME SAUCE

A creamy, rich and nutty sauce that's completely plant-based and without nuts. It works perfectly with the shabu shabu on page 121, as a dip for raw or blanched vegetables.

MAKES ABOUT 250ML (1 CUP)

about 120g (½ cup) Japanese sesame paste or tahini
4 tsp sugar
1 tsp salt
3 tbsp Japanese soy sauce
6 tbsp water or dashi (see page 19)
3 tsp rice vinegar

PREPARATION

1. If you have a hand-held blender, place all of the ingredients in a tall beaker and whizz until you get a smooth sauce. Otherwise, place the sesame paste, sugar, and salt in a large bowl, pour in a little liquid at a time and whisk to form a thick, smooth sauce. Keeps for 1 week in the fridge.

Goma dressing

SESAME DRESSING

Dilute gomadare (see left) with a little oil and acid, and you have yourself a lighter, slightly acidic dressing. The umami and creaminess adds variation to a classic side salad.

MAKES ABOUT 200ML (SCANT 1 CUP)

1 tbsp rice vinegar
1 tbsp sesame oil
2 tbsp rapeseed (canola) oil
4 tbsp gomadare (see left)
1 tsp sugar
⅓ tsp salt
1 tbsp toasted sesame seeds
1 tbsp water

PREPARATION

1. Mix the vinegar with both the oils in a jug (pitcher).
2. Place the gomadare, sugar, salt, and sesame seeds in a large bowl and add the oil mixture in a thin stream while whisking.
3. Adjust the consistency by pouring in the water towards the end. Keeps for a few days in the fridge.

Otsumami

QUICK DISHES MADE FROM USEFUL BASIC SAUCES

おつまみ

My useful basic sauces will help you make simple small accompaniments to serve with any dish. Just choose different vegetables, fish, or meat to taste.

DEEP FRY AUBERGINE (EGGPLANT) slices and top with finely grated ginger and sliced spring onions (scallions). Drizzle with tare and taberu rayu.

BLANCH GREEN BEANS in salted water and mix with gomadare. Sprinkle with toasted sesame seeds.

BLANCH A WHOLE TOMATO for 5 seconds. Leave to cool, and peel. Cut a cross in the top of the tomato and drizzle over some ponzu, taberu rayu (just the oil) and olive oil or sesame oil.

FINELY SLICE SOME BABY/SILVERSKIN ONIONS and place in iced water. Dry and top with some katsuobushi and ponzu.

MAKE A FEW SLASHES ON THE SURFACE OF KING TRUMPET/OYSTER MUSHROOMS (or any other mushrooms) and fry in oil in a frying pan until cooked through. Brush with tare to glaze.

BLANCH BEANSPROUTS for 5 seconds in boiling salted water. Top with taberu rayu (with the bits) and ponzu.

Dashi

だし

JAPANESE STOCK

Dashi is a bit like tea. Think about the temperature and infuse gently to get the best taste from the first brewing. Then you can enjoy it again after a second brewing. For me, luxury is drinking freshly-brewed dashi with just a pinch of salt. It gives umami in both flavour and aroma. Don't forget to save the kombu and katsuobushi after brewing. You can eat them as simple accompaniments rather than discarding these high-quality ingredients.

Ichiban dashi

DASHI WITH KOMBU & KATSUOBUSHI

It takes about an hour to make dashi. It can feel overwhelming to get home from work and make the stock before you can prepare dinner – especially with hungry kids – so you can use the dashi in powder form that's available from Asian grocery shops (you simply dissolve this in hot water), but if you do have time, make your own stock. Remember that you can be generous with the quantities of kombu and katsuobushi so their unique flavours come through. But be careful with the temperature when making the stock. This recipe works really well when made in large quantities and frozen for future use.

MAKES ABOUT 1.6 LITRES (6½ CUPS)
2 litres (8½ cups) cold water
30g (1oz) kombu, in large pieces
30g (1oz) katsuobushi

PREPARATION

1. Place the water and kombu in a saucepan for 10 minutes without heat.
2. Turn the heat on low and allow the kombu to soak in the water until bubbles start to form on the surface and on the bottom and edge of the saucepan. Allow to bubble gently for 15 minutes without boiling. Remove the kombu.
3. Increase the heat. Just when the liquid is starting to boil, add the katsuobushi and turn off the heat immediately.
4. Wait until the katsuobushi has infused and sinks to the bottom of the pan.
5. Carefully pass the stock through a strainer or kitchen paper (paper towel). Leave to drain properly and do not squeeze out the katsuobushi. The stock keeps for 5 days in the fridge and 1 month in the freezer.

Make the most of used kombu and katsuobushi...

Ichiban means "first", so ichiban dashi is the first dashi. Then there is niban dashi – the second dashi. You make this by placing the kombu and katsuobushi from the ichiban dashi into a saucepan of cold water and bringing it to the boil, then simmering for a while before straining it.

The first dashi is transparent, with a pure, elegant flavour, while the second is cloudy with a more robust flavour but still with plenty of umami. In restaurants in Japan, ichiban dashi is usually served as a garnished broth or in dishes where udon are served hot and the flavour of the dashi itself can emerge. Meanwhile, niban dashi is used as a base for stews and batters for other dishes, where additional flavours will be combined with the stock.

However, it can be a bit awkward to have such a large quantity of different variations of dashi in your home. So here are two great accompaniments to eat with rice, which you can make instead of the second dashi.

Okobu
STEWED KOMBU

MAKES ABOUT 100G (3½OZ)
kombu from 1 batch ichiban dashi
    (see page 19), squeezed
300ml (1¼ cups) water
3½ tbsp Japanese soy sauce
3½ tbsp mirin
2 tbsp sake
½ tbsp sugar

PREPARATION
1. Finely shred the kombu.
2. Place all of the ingredients in a saucepan, bring to the boil, and simmer over a low heat for about 30–40 minutes until the kombu is soft and the liquid is almost boiled away.
3. Eat as it is with rice, or mix with sesame seeds. See also the recipe for Onigiri on page 69.

Okaka
FRIED KATSUOBUSHI

MAKES ABOUT 100G (3½OZ)
1 tbsp rapeseed (canola) oil
katsuobushi from 1 batch ichiban dashi,
    (see page 19), squeezed
½ tbsp sesame oil
1 tbsp mirin
1 tbsp Japanese soy sauce
salt

PREPARATION
1. Heat the rapeseed oil in a frying pan. Break up the katsuobushi as well as you can and fry in the pan, stirring constantly. When it starts to get crispy, add the sesame oil and a small pinch of salt, and fry for another few minutes.
2. When the katsuobushi is crisp, turn off the heat and add the mirin and soy sauce. Eat with rice, sprinkle over salads, or see the recipe for Onigiri on page 69.

Nama tamago
RAW EGGS

Japanese people like to use raw eggs in many different dishes. They produce a creaminess that works very well with soy sauce-based flavours, such as freshly cooked rice or udon noodles with egg yolk and a splash of soy sauce. Or you can dip meat in raw egg, like in Sukiyaki on page 118, or use one to top Gyudon (see page 56).

Onsen tamago
HOT-SPRING EGGS

This preparation method originates in an area of Japan where there are many hot springs, and exploits the fact that while egg yolks set at 65°C (149°F), egg whites only set at 75°C (167°F). People began cooking eggs in the hot springs, where the water was around 65°C. This produced a creamy egg yolk and a soft, semi-runny white. Since then, these eggs have become popular all over the country.

6 eggs, straight from the fridge

PREPARATION
1. Bring 1.5 litres (6¼ cups) of water to the boil in a saucepan. Turn off the heat and pour in 300ml (1¼ cups) of cold water. Add the eggs (the water should cover the eggs) and replace the lid.
2. Leave to stand for 20–30 minutes at room temperature. Lift the eggs out of the water and crack before using.

Yude tamago
BOILED EGGS

Cook your eggs by placing them in boiling water. Add the eggs carefully and adjust the heat so the water is simmering steadily (remember that the temperature of the water always falls when you cook several eggs simultaneously). Cook the eggs for about 7 minutes depending on size. If the eggs are at room temperature, you may want to cook them for 30–60 seconds less.

Zuke tamago
MARINATED EGGS

Marinate shelled boiled eggs to give them more flavour. Eat as they are or use to garnish rice or noodle dishes. If you're only going to cook a few eggs, you can halve the quantity of tare. The used tare can be reheated and served with other dishes, or it can be saved for future marinades.

1 batch tare (see page 13)
2 star anise
any number of boiled eggs (see Intro)

PREPARATION
1. Make your tare, adding the 2 star anise along with the mirin and sake (see page 13). If you're using saved tare, you can simply reheat it with the star anise. Pour the sauce and star anise into a bowl and allow to cool.
2. Shell the eggs and leave them in the tare for 1 hour at room temperature, then turn the eggs and marinate for a further 1 hour. They are ready to eat at this point, but they can marinate for up to 2 days in the fridge. This will make them firmer and browner with more flavour. Remove the marinated eggs from the fridge in good time for them to reach room temperature before serving.

24

Noodles

When Japanese people say "noodles", many people shout RAMEN! Despite the fact that ramen is originally from China, the Japanese developed many of their own variants very early on, and ramen has become a key element in the Japanese food culture that is so popular all over the world. But other noodles, like soba and udon, have long been present in Japanese cuisine. Unlike ramen, these are milder and less greasy, but still very moreish. A large bowl of udon or soba in dashi (with whatever toppings you have to hand) for brunch on a cold weekend, as a morning-after breakfast, or for dinner after a long day, is a comforting, restorative dish. All of these recipes are easy to make at home.

Chicken stock

鶏だし

BASIC RECIPE

Ramen is delicious, but sometimes it can feel like too big a project to make it at home. This easy basic stock works well to make a simpler version of home-made ramen that doesn't require you to spend many hours cooking up a huge saucepan of broth or dealing with a chicken carcass. You can use this basic recipe to make many different variations of ramen, which you'll find over the following pages.

MAKES 1.5 LITRES (6¼ CUPS)

2 litres (8½ cups) water
2 garlic cloves, sliced
6 thin slices of ginger
2 x 10cm (4in) pieces of kombu
5 dried shiitake mushrooms, torn in half
2½ tsp salt
700g (1lb 9oz) boneless skin-on chicken thighs or boneless chicken breasts

PREPARATION

1. Place all of the ingredients except the chicken in a large saucepan. Bring to the boil.
2. While you wait for it to boil, you can check your chicken pieces. If they aren't all the same size, or have thicker parts, make a few slashes in them so they open up and cook as evenly as possible.
3. When the liquid in the saucepan is boiling properly, add all of the chicken pieces, making sure they aren't overlapping. Wait until the liquid has come to a simmer again, then turn off the heat and cover. Leave to stand for 40 minutes at room temperature.
4. Remove the chicken and reserve, then bring the liquid to the boil again and skim. Strain the stock.
5. Now you have an elegant chicken stock, and also juicy cooked chicken that you can use with different variations of ramen.

Shoyu ramen

醤油ラーメン

RAMEN WITH SOY SAUCE

This is a a version of ramen using shoyu (Japanese soy sauce). Here, the mixing of chicken stock and dashi gives depth and enhances the flavours of the soy sauce.

SERVES 4

2 tbsp rapeseed (canola) oil
2 tsp sesame oil
1 tsp finely grated garlic
1 tsp salt
4 tbsp Japanese soy sauce
300ml (1¼ cups) chicken stock (see page 27)
200ml (scant 1 cup) dashi (see page 19), or extra chicken stock
280g (10oz) dried noodles, or 500g (1lb 2oz) fresh

TOPPING SUGGESTIONS

2 chicken fillets from making the stock, sliced and reheated
4 marinated or boiled eggs (see page 23)
2 spring onions (scallions), finely sliced
150g (5½oz) beansprouts, blanched in salted water and mixed with 2 tsp sesame oil
taberu rayu (see page 14)

PREPARATION

1. Mix the rapeseed oil, sesame oil, garlic, salt, and soy sauce in a small saucepan over a medium heat until it starts to bubble properly and you can see the soy sauce beginning to stick to the bottom. Allow to boil for a further 20 seconds, stirring constantly.
2. Remove from the heat and continue to stir gently until it stops bubbling, then pour the soy sauce mixture into a larger saucepan together with the stock and dashi. Set aside.
3. Bring a separate large saucepan of water to the boil and boil the noodles for 1 minute less than it says on the packet (they will continue cooking in the hot stock). Strain the noodles and thoroughly shake off the water.
4. Bring the stock to the boil and then pour into 4 warm bowls. Carefully divide the noodles between the bowls and add your toppings of choice.

TOP TIPS! If you use dried noodles, rinse the boiled noodles in cold water until they have cooled completely. Strain the noodles thoroughly then heat them up in the stock. This is an extra step but gives the noodles more bite.

If you don't have any noodles at home, you can boil some capellini (thin spaghetti) in water containing 1½ tablespoons of bicarbonate of soda (baking soda). They taste remarkably similar to ramen noodles!

Shio ramen

塩ラーメン

RAMEN WITH SALT

This is the easiest version of ramen, and you can choose from many different toppings. For example, this stock works very well with meat, fish, shellfish, or fried vegetables.

SERVES 4

500ml (2 cups) chicken stock (see page 27)
2 tsp salt
1 tbsp fish sauce
280g (10oz) dried noodles, or 500g (1lb 2oz) fresh

TOPPING SUGGESTIONS

2 chicken fillets from making the stock, sliced and reheated
4 marinated or boiled eggs (see page 23)
2 spring onions (scallions), shredded
yuzu kosho and/or taberu rayu (see page 14)

PREPARATION

1. Heat the stock in a saucepan and season with the salt and fish sauce.
2. Bring a separate large saucepan of water to the boil and boil the noodles for 1–1½ minutes less than the instructions on the packet (they will continue to cook in the hot stock). Strain the noodles and thoroughly shake off the water.
3. Bring the stock to the boil and then pour into 4 warm bowls. Carefully divide the noodles between the bowls and add your toppings of choice.

TOP TIP! **You can heat the noodle bowls by rinsing them in hot water or pouring hot water into them.**

Miso tsukemen

味噌つけ麺

DIPPING NOODLES WITH MISO

Tsukemen is a dish where noodles and sauce are served separately. You dip the noodles into the sauce before every bite. The sauce should have a slightly thicker consistency than regular ramen broth, so it coats and sticks to the noodles when you dip them.

SERVES 4

15g (½oz) katsuobushi
600ml (generous 2½ cups) chicken stock (see page 27)
280g (10oz) dried noodles, or 500g (1lb 2oz) fresh, cooked and drained

FOR THE DIPPING SAUCE BASE
3 tsp finely grated garlic
3 tsp finely grated ginger
3 tbsp mirin
3 tbsp miso
3 tbsp Japanese soy sauce
3 tbsp muscovado sugar
3 tbsp sesame oil
3 tbsp rapeseed (canola) oil
1½ tsp gochujang (Korean chilli paste)
2 tsp white sesame paste or tahini

TOPPING SUGGESTIONS
4 Onsen Tamago (see page 23)
2 chicken fillets from making the stock, sliced and reheated
2 spring onions (scallions), finely sliced
shredded nori

PREPARATION

1. Place all the ingredients for the dipping sauce in a saucepan and warm over a medium heat, stirring constantly. Reduce the heat when the sauce begins to bubble and splatter, then simmer, while stirring, until the sauce begins to stick on the bottom of the pan and the flavours are concentrated.
2. Crush the katsuobushi as finely as possible in a plastic bag or mortar and pestle, and add to the sauce base.
3. Dilute the base with one third of the hot stock and whisk, or preferably mix with a hand-held blender. Carefully add the rest of the stock and stir until no lumps remain.
4. Bring to the boil, then reduce the heat and simmer for 2 minutes. Whizz with a hand-held blender for about 30 seconds until everything is combined and the broth takes on a slightly creamy consistency.
5. Divide the broth and the onsen eggs (if using) between 4 bowls, and serve the noodles, chicken, and any other accompaniments on 4 plates on the side.

Nuku udon
Nuku soba

ぬくうどん

ぬくそば

HOT UDON & HOT SOBA

A simple pleasure – the flavour and aroma of great dashi and noodles. In lots of places, people tend to eat kebabs after a night out, but I think most Japanese people would agree that this dish makes you feel relaxed and comforted. Exactly what you need when you've drunk too much. Wakame is an edible seaweed that's often sold salted, dried, or frozen in Asian food shops.

SERVES 4

280g (10oz) dried udon or soba noodles, or 500g (1lb 2oz) fresh
600ml (generous 2½ cups) dashi (see page 19), or use shop-bought
1 tbsp Japanese soy sauce
1 tbsp mirin
1 tsp salt

TOPPING SUGGESTIONS

5 spring onions (scallions), finely sliced
4 onsen tamago or nama tamago (see page 23)
wakame, soaked in cold water until soft (no more than 3 minutes), then squeezed
shichimi togarashi
yuzu kosho

1. Bring a large saucepan of unsalted water to the boil and cook the noodles according to the packet instructions.
2. Meanwhile, pour the dashi, soy sauce, mirin, and salt into another saucepan, and bring to the boil.
3. Divide the noodles between 4 bowls and pour over the dashi. Top with spring onions, eggs, and wakame, and serve with shichimi togarashi and yuzu kosho on the side, if using.

Hiyashichuka

冷やし中華

SUMMER NOODLES

When all the ramen restaurants begin proclaiming "We have hiyashichuka!", you know summer has arrived. Hiyashichuka is a cold noodle dish that's normally only served in the summer. Try it out one day when it's far too hot and you have no appetite. It also works really well to switch your vegetables with whatever is in season. For the best experience, it's important to prepare all the components in plenty of time so they can be served chilled.

SERVES 4

280g (10oz) dried noodles, or 500g (1lb 2oz) fresh
Japanese karashi mustard or Dijon mustard, to serve

FOR THE SAUCE

200ml (scant 1 cup) tare (see page 13)
4 tbsp rice vinegar
1 tsp finely grated ginger
1 tsp finely grated garlic
1 tsp sesame oil

FOR THE USUYAKI TAMAGO (THIN FRIED EGG)

6 eggs
1 tbsp mirin
½ tsp salt
½ tsp Japanese soy sauce
oil, for frying

FOR THE TOPPINGS

200g (7oz) beansprouts
sesame oil
1 cucumber, cut into thin strips
3 tomatoes, cut into wedges
150g (5½oz) cooked ham or chicken, finely sliced
3 spring onions (scallions), finely shredded
4 sheets of nori, cut into pieces

PREPARATION

1. FOR THE SAUCE: Mix all the sauce ingredients in a small jug (pitcher) or bowl and set aside.
2. FOR THE USUYAKI TAMAGO: Mix the eggs, mirin, salt, and soy sauce in a large bowl. Heat a little oil in a frying pan, then fry the batter, a little at a time, to make pancakes that are as thin as possible. Fry on both sides without allowing the pancakes to colour. Allow to cool a little before placing them on top of each other. When all of the pancakes are fried, shred them finely. Set aside.
3. Bring a large saucepan of water to the boil. Place the beansprouts in a sieve and rest the sieve in the water for 30 seconds to blanch the beansprouts, then lift up and leave to drain. Tip the beansprouts into a bowl and mix with 2 teaspoons of sesame oil.
4. Save the cooking water and cook the noodles according to the instructions on the packet. As soon as they are cooked, plunge them into iced water to cool, then drain thoroughly and shake off any excess water. Drizzle over a few drops of sesame oil so the noodles don't stick together.
5. Place the noodles in the bottom of 4 bowls and add your toppings. Pour over a few spoonfuls of sauce and serve with a little mustard on the side. Or you can serve the dish by placing all the accompaniments in separate bowls and letting your guests serve themselves.

Yakisoba

焼きそば

FRIED NOODLES

This is a classic dish that can often be bought from street stalls during festivals in Japan. The noodles are usually cooked on a griddle and coated in sauce. If you're going to make four portions, I recommend that you use a frying pan 27cm (11in) in diameter. If you don't have one that big, it's better to cook in batches. For the best results, fry the noodles, and vegetables separately and mix them at the end.

SERVES 4

- 10 slices of bacon, cut into 3cm (1¼in)-wide pieces
- 5 tbsp rapeseed (canola) oil
- 2 large onions, cut into thin wedges
- 4 × 5cm (2in) pieces of carrot, halved lengthways and sliced
- 130g (4½oz) fresh white or hispi cabbage, sliced
- 1 tbsp sesame oil
- 400g (14oz) egg noodles, cooked and drained
- 1 tsp finely grated ginger
- 1 tsp finely grated garlic
- 100ml (scant ½ cup) bannou sauce (see page 13)
- 1½ tbsp Japanese soy sauce
- freshly ground black pepper

TO SERVE

- mayonnaise
- katsuobushi
- aonori (seaweed powder)
- beni shoga (pickled shredded red ginger)

PREPARATION

1. Heat a frying pan over a medium heat and fry the bacon. Place in a large bowl and set aside.
2. Pour 2 tablespoons of the rapeseed oil into the same pan and fry the onions and carrots until cooked through, then add the cabbage and fry until soft. Add to the bowl containing the bacon.
3. Quickly wipe the pan with kitchen paper (paper towel) and heat up again with the remaining 3 tablespoons of rapeseed oil and the sesame oil. Add the noodles, together with the ginger and garlic, and fry briefly, stirring often.
4. When the noodles are warm and smell nicely of ginger and garlic, add the bannou sauce, soy sauce and a few twists of black pepper. Stir to ensure the ingredients are mixed properly.
5. Tip the bacon and vegetables back into the pan with the noodles, turn off the heat, and mix well. Serve on 4 plates, topped with the mayonnaise, katsuobushi, seaweed powder, and pickled ginger.

Rice

There are over 100,000 varieties of rice. They can mainly be divided into three different types: japonica, indica, and javanica. In Japan, we traditionally eat japonica, also called round-grain or sticky rice, which has a shorter, rounder appearance and is slightly sticky with starch. When cooked, it develops a particular scent and sweetness, and becomes glossy. And it's very tasty!

Rice has long been a big part of Japanese culture. Many traditional Japanese festivals are based on prayers for a good rice harvest, and long ago people even paid their taxes in rice.

One of my favourite food experiences, even though it's a recurring feature of everyday life, is when the steam brings with it the smell of freshly cooked rice from the rice cooker. When I'm asked which is my favourite Japanese dish, I always say rice balls (onigiri). Then the other person often looks at me curiously and asks whether there's any special filling I most prefer. But no, in my memory the best dish I've ever eaten is my grandmother's shio-nigiri – a rice ball made of very freshly cooked rice with a little sprinkle of salt and a piece of nori. The fluffiest and most comforting onigiri there is!

Boiled rice

炊飯

If you can, use Japanese round-grain (sticky) rice. There are many different varieties. In Japan, we usually say that the rice should be soaked for 30 minutes after washing in the summer, and for 60 minutes in the winter. This is because the water temperature affects how quickly the rice absorbs the water. If you're short of time, you can boil the rice immediately after washing it (if you do this, add 10 per cent more water), but it's when you soak it properly that you understand how delicious rice can be.

You can cook a large batch at once, divide it into portions and freeze it. Then all you need to do is remove it and microwave or steam it quickly before serving.

PREPARATION

1. Wash your rice in water in a large bowl. Change the water a few times until it's no longer cloudy, then pour off all the water, ideally through a sieve.

IN A RICE COOKER

Add your rice and water. For 240g (1¼ cups) rice, you'll need 300–350ml (1¼–1½ cups) water, and 300ml (1¼ cups) water if you want to make sushi rice. Leave the rice in the water for at least 30 minutes, then turn on the rice cooker according to the instructions and leave it on until the rice is ready.

IN A SAUCEPAN

Place your rice and water into a lidded saucepan. For 240g (1¼ cups) rice, you'll need 350ml (1½ cups) water, and 300ml (1¼ cups) water if you want to make sushi rice. Leave the rice in the water for at least 30 minutes, then place over a medium heat and bring to the boil with the lid on. Reduce the heat to low and cook for 10 minutes. Turn off the heat and leave to stand for 10 minutes with the lid on. Remove the lid and place the saucepan over a high heat for 30–40 seconds to remove the moisture from the bottom. The rice is ready to eat.

Omuraisu

オムライス

OMELETTE & RICE

Omelette + rice = omrice (omuraisu). Just as the name implies, this is a dish made from rice rolled in a thin omelette. This is a classic dish made from rice mixed with vegetables and chicken, and flavoured with ketchup. It's very popular in Japan and there are many different versions. Here I make one that uses mushrooms instead of chicken. Use low-sugar ketchup if you can, as it gives a pleasant acidity to the dish.

This is a simplified method for the perfect omelette where you shape the rice and simply lay the creamy omelette on top.

SERVES 4

FOR THE RICE
500g (1lb 2oz) cooked round-grain (sticky) rice (see page 47)
1 tbsp rapeseed (canola) oil
1 tbsp butter
90g (3¼oz) white or chestnut (cremini) mushrooms, finely chopped
2 tsp finely grated garlic
80g (2¾oz) onion, finely chopped
80g (2¾oz) carrot, finely chopped
80g (2¾oz) green (bell) pepper, finely chopped
4 tbsp mirin
½ tsp salt
1 tbsp Japanese soy sauce
4 tbsp ketchup

FOR THE OMELETTE
8 eggs
3½ tbsp double (heavy) cream
1½ tsp salt
butter, for frying

FOR THE SAUCE (OR KETCHUP)
5 tbsp tomato purée (paste)
4 tbsp mirin
4 tbsp sake or dry white wine
1 tbsp Japanese soy sauce

PREPARATION

1. If using cooked and cooled rice, reheat the boiled rice in the microwave or in a steamer.
2. FOR THE SAUCE: Mix the ingredients for the sauce in a bowl and set aside. (You can also choose to use regular ketchup instead of making a sauce from scratch.)
3. FOR THE RICE: Heat the oil and butter in a pan over a medium heat. First fry the mushrooms until they have browned and smell good, then add the garlic, onion, carrot, and green pepper and allow to cook through. This won't take long.
4. Add the mirin, salt, soy sauce, and ketchup, and cook for a few minutes.
5. Add the rice to the saucepan and stir. Be careful not to break the rice grains. Turn off the heat.
6. Spoon a quarter of the rice mixture into a rice bowl, press lightly, and turn out onto a plate. Remove the bowl carefully to keep the domed shape. Repeat with the rest of the rice.
7. FOR THE OMELETTE: Whisk together the eggs, cream, and salt into a smooth batter and divide it into 4 portions. Warm a frying pan (ideally 20cm/8in in diameter) over a medium heat and add a small knob of butter. Once the butter has melted, pour a portion of the egg mixture into the pan and tilt the pan to evenly distribute the batter. At the same time, stir the surface with chopsticks or a fork. It should be a little like scrambled eggs, with a thin skin on the bottom.
8. Tilt the pan and use a spatula to help the egg mixture slide out of the pan and over the shaped rice until it is covered. Repeat with the remaining batter and rice.
9. Pour over some of the sauce, or eat with ketchup. If you manage to make a really creamy omelette, it tastes really good just as it is.

Donburi

どんぶり

A LARGE BOWL WITH RICE

The word donburi comes from a large, deep bowl that can hold enough food to fill you up. It's also the name of the dish that is usually served in this bowl – rice topped with different kinds of meat or vegetables. The various types of donburi are distinguished by calling them the name of the topping + "don". Here I bring you two versions: oyako (chicken and egg) don, and gyu (steak) don.

Oyako don

親子丼

RICE WITH CHICKEN & EGGS

Oyako means "parents and children". Here, chicken and eggs are used together in one dish. Use a high-sided 27cm (11in)-diameter frying pan or a smaller one but cook in two batches. (In Japanese restaurants, each serving is cooked in its own pan for the best results.) The pan also needs a suitable lid.

SERVES 4

190g (6¾oz) onion, finely sliced
2 spring onions (scallions), finely sliced, white and green parts separated
250g (9oz) boneless chicken legs, with or without skin, cut into slices/bite-sized pieces
6 eggs
4 portions freshly boiled round-grain (sticky) rice (see page 47)
shichimi or sansho pepper (optional)
salt

FOR THE SAUCE

250ml (1 cup) dashi (see page 19), or use shop-bought
2 tbsp mirin
2 tbsp Japanese soy sauce
1 tsp finely grated ginger
½ tsp salt

PREPARATION

1. FOR THE SAUCE: Put all the sauce ingredients in a frying pan and cook over a high heat.
2. Put the onion and the white parts of the spring onions in the sauce and cook for 1 minute with the lid on. Salt the chicken pieces lightly and add them to the pan. Fry for 1–2 minutes, stir, then replace the lid and cook for another 1–2 minutes.
3. Beat the eggs briefly with a fork and add a little salt. Remove the lid from the pan and increase the heat so the liquid is boiling properly. Drizzle the egg mixture into the pan and stir with chopsticks in a zigzag motion from one side of the pan to the other. Reduce the heat to low, replace the lid and simmer for 2–3 minutes. Turn off the heat and leave to stand with the lid on for another 1–2 minutes until the eggs have just solidified but are still a little loose.
4. Divide the rice between 4 bowls, top with the chicken and egg mixture and the green parts of the spring onions, and serve with a little shichimi pepper (if using).

Drizzle the egg mixture in a thin stream using chopsticks, then stir with the chopsticks in a zigzag movement from one side of the pan to the other.

Gyudon

RICE WITH BEEF

牛丼

Gyu means beef. This is a very simple dish, but it's important to work quickly as you prepare it to get the perfect consistency in both meat and onions. If you read through the recipe and have all the ingredients ready before you start, it's quite straightforward.

Use a frying pan about 27cm (11in) wide for four portions of meat. If you have a smaller pan, you can fry the meat in batches. In Japan, you can buy super-thin pre-sliced meat, but that isn't available everywhere. If you have a really sharp knife, you can cut it as thinly as possible (you don't have to end up with completely round slices, but aim to make them extra thin). If you have a cutting machine, you can slightly freeze the meat and then cut it into slices about 1mm thick.

SERVES 4

500g (1lb 2oz) entrecôte or braising steak, finely sliced (see Intro)
4 portions freshly boiled round-grain (sticky) rice (see page 47)
1 tbsp rapeseed (canola) oil
260g (9¼oz) onion, cut into thin wedges
1 tsp finely grated garlic
1 tsp finely grated ginger
½ tbsp sesame oil
4 egg yolks (optional)
gari (pickled ginger) or beni shoga (pickled shredded red ginger); optional
freshly ground black pepper

FOR THE SAUCE (OR USE 150G/5OZ TARE, SEE PAGE 13)
6 tbsp Japanese soy sauce
4 tbsp mirin
4 tbsp sake
4 tsp muscovado sugar

PREPARATION

1. FOR THE SAUCE: Mix together all the sauce ingredients and set aside.
2. Heat a large frying pan with rapeseed oil over a high heat until it starts to smoke.
3. Place the meat slices in the pan, making sure they don't overlap. If you don't have a big enough pan, you can fry the meat in batches. Don't reduce the heat, but allow the meat to fry until it's nicely browned on one side. Don't move or turn the slices. Then lift the meat onto a plate and grind over the pepper. It should be only partially cooked.
4. Leave the pan on the heat and add the onion, garlic, ginger, and sesame oil. Turn off the heat and stir until the pan stops sizzling.
5. Add the sauce, saving a few spoonfuls, and turn the heat up to high again. Allow to fry for 1 minute.
6. Return the meat to the pan and remove from the heat once more. The meat will be nicely cooked by the residual heat. If you have thicker slices, you can allow the meat to cook for a minute before turning off the heat, but be careful not to overcook.
7. Put the rice in 4 bowls and top with the meat. Pour over the rest of the sauce.
8. If you want, you can serve it with an egg yolk on top and a little pickled ginger.

Temakizushi

手巻き寿司

HOME-MADE SUSHI

This home-made version of sushi uses ingredients that are easy to find in supermarkets. It can be nice to make luxurious sushi, with fresh fish and shellfish, but what you put on the rice and nori is completely up to you. For example, as a child, my brothers and I had sausages and fried meat pieces with shiso and mayonnaise.

SERVES 4

about 300g (10½oz) raw fish, such as salmon, tuna, trout roe, scallops, turbot
240g (1¼ cups) round-grain (sticky) rice
100ml (scant ½ cup) sushi-su vinegar (see below), or use shop-bought

FOR THE SUSHI-SU VINEGAR
200ml (scant 1 cup) rice vinegar
3½ tbsp sugar
2 tsp salt
5cm (2in) piece of kombu

FOR THE POACHED SHIITAKE
6 large shiitake mushrooms
3½ tbsp Japanese soy sauce
3½ tbsp mirin
1 tbsp sugar

TO SERVE
1 packet nori, cut into 10cm (4in) squares
1 Dashimaki Tamago (see page 139), shredded
½ cucumber, shredded
shiso leaves or shiso cress (optional)
wasabi
gari (pickled ginger)
Japanese soy sauce

PREPARATION

1. FOR THE SUSHI-SU VINEGAR: Heat the ingredients in a saucepan and allow to melt together. Leave to cool, then remove the kombu and set the vinegar aside.
2. FOR THE POACHED SHIITAKE: Shred the mushrooms, then simmer them with the soy sauce, mirin, and sugar in a saucepan until the liquid has almost boiled away. Leave to cool.
3. Cut all the fish into strips about 1cm (½in) thick or into slices about 5mm (¼in) thick.
4. Meanwhile, cook the rice (see page 47) and mix it with the 100ml (scant ½ cup) sushi-su vinegar in a large, wide bowl while still hot. Use a spatula or rice paddle and stir with "cutting" movements to prevent the grains from being mashed. Cover the rice with a damp tea (dish) towel and leave to stand for at least 10 minutes before serving.
5. Place all the ingredients in bowls or on plates and set them on the table.
6. Homemade sushi is eaten a little like tacos. Place some rice on a sheet of nori, top with your choice of other ingredients and roll into a small package. Dip in soy sauce and enjoy!

TOP TIP! Save any remaining sushi-su vinegar for the next time you make sushi, or use it to pickle vegetables.

Chazuke

茶漬け

RICE IN TEA

There are many different rice dishes with broth, but chazuke is completely unique to Japan and combines rice with tea. There are different types of Japanese tea, and my favourites are a green tea like sencha or a roasted green tea like hojicha. With hojicha, it's traditional to top the rice with only umeboshi and nori. This is a dish that's easy to prepare but still feels indulgent and warms the stomach. You can also make a version with dashi.

Shake ikura chazuke

鮭いくら茶漬け

RICE IN TEA WITH SALMON & SALMON ROE

A simple but indulgent version of chazuke with cookese salmon (shake) and roe.

SERVES 4

300g (10½oz) salmon fillet
1½ tsp salt
50g (1¾oz) trout or salmon roe
1 tbsp Japanese soy sauce
rapeseed (canola) oil, for frying
4 portions freshly boiled round-grain (sticky) rice (see page 47)
4 tbsp arare (Japanese puffed rice)
15g (½oz) spring onions (scallions), finely sliced
1–2 sheets of nori, finely shredded
wasabi
800ml (generous 3½ cups) Japanese sencha (light green tea) or dashi

PREPARATION

1. Rub the salmon thoroughly with the salt, then leave to stand for at least 15 minutes at room temperature.
2. Mix the trout roe with the soy sauce and set aside.
3. Dry the salmon with kitchen paper (paper towel). Heat a little rapeseed oil in a frying pan over a medium heat and fry the salmon until it is cooked through. Leave to cool and then flake the salmon into pieces. It should be quite salty.
4. Divide your freshly cooked rice between 4 bowls and top with the salmon, trout roe, arare, spring onions, and nori, and add a small dollop of wasabi.
5. Heat the tea thoroughly and pour over the rice to serve. Eat with a spoon.

Zuke chazuke

RICE IN TEA WITH MARINATED FISH

漬け茶漬け

An excellent quick lunch or supper.

SERVES 4

250g (9oz) fish that can be eaten raw (salmon, mackerel, scallops), in 2mm (1/16in)-thick slices

FOR THE MARINADE
4 tbsp miso
2 tbsp mirin
1 tbsp sugar
1 tbsp Japanese soy sauce
1 tsp sesame oil
1 tsp finely grated ginger

TO SERVE
4 portions freshly boiled round-grain (sticky) rice (see page 47)
30g (1oz) spring onions (scallions), shredded
4 tbsp toasted white sesame seeds
10g (⅓oz) daikon cress or cress
4 tbsp arare (Japanese puffed rice); optional
wasabi
800ml (generous 3½ cups) sencha tea or dashi (see page 19)

PREPARATION

1. Mix together all the ingredients for the marinade and rub into the fish. Leave to stand for 10 minutes at room temperature.
2. Place your freshly boiled rice in bowls and top with the marinated fish, spring onions, sesame seeds, cress, and puffed rice (if using), and a small dollop of wasabi.
3. Heat the tea thoroughly and pour over the rice bowls to serve.

Onigiri

おにぎり

RICE BALLS

For me, onigiri is real soul food. As a child, I took onigiri with me on weekend activities, picnics or when my family went on car journeys. I remember when I was 17 I was feeling sad and, with little appetite, I would shut myself in my bedroom to be alone. But one day my mother's best friend came to visit. As soon as she heard of my sadness, she made me onigiri with fish, nori, and sesame. I still remember the feeling when I ate the first onigiri. My tears began to fall and my body was started to feel warm all over. I felt so much love in those little rice balls she had made, in the energy inside me. I will never forget it. And for the rest of my life I will wrap as many onigiri as my daughter needs.

MAKES AS MANY AS YOU LIKE

freshly boiled rice (see page 47)
choice of filling, if using, such as okobu or okaka (see page 20), or umeboshi
sheets of nori, cut to the size you need (I usually divide a sheet first in the middle and then each half into 3 pieces, so I get 6 pieces per sheet)
salt

ONIGIRI WITHOUT FILLING

1. Add a portion of rice to a rice bowl – I usually use about a handful. (Freshly cooked rice is very hot, but if you can stand it, it always makes a nice, airy rice ball.)
2. Shake the bowl slightly until the rice begins to form and hold together in the bowl. Moisten one hand with cold water and sprinkle a little fine salt into your palm.
3. Turn the rice out onto your hand and gently press into a triangle shape. Don't press too hard – the rice grains on the surface should still be intact.
4. Take a piece of nori and wrap it around the rice ball. You have now made a simple shio-nigiri.

ONIGIRI WITH FILLING

1. Add a portion of rice to a rice bowl – I usually use about a handful. (Freshly cooked rice is very hot, but if you can stand it, it always makes a nice, airy rice ball.)
2. Shake the bowl slightly until the rice begins to form and hold together in the bowl. Make a small hole with your thumb in the middle of the rice, add your filling and cover with a little more rice. Moisten one hand with cold water and sprinkle a little fine salt into your palm.
3. Turn the rice out onto your hand and gently press into a triangle shape. Don't press too hard – the rice grains on the surface should still be intact.
4. Take a piece of nori and wrap it around the rice ball. You have now made a filled nigiri. If you like, you can top it with a little extra filling.

ONIGIRI BY HAND

ONIGIRI USING A MOULD

Deep fried

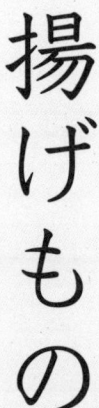

Here are my recipes for some popular deep-fried dishes. Deep frying isn't actually that complicated, and it's no problem to get hold of the ingredients. I have a few top tips for achieving a nice crispy surface when you're deep frying at home:

1. Don't skimp on the oil. Dealing with the oil after frying can feel like a chore, which means that many people do their "deep" frying in as little oil as possible, but unfortunately this doesn't produce the best results. I recommend being generous with the oil.
2. Maintain the right temperature. In the recipes, I give a slightly higher temperature than you actually need, because the oil temperature falls when you add ingredients. It's also a good idea to check the temperature of the oil while you're frying. Increase the heat if the temperature falls.
3. Don't fry too much at the same time, as this will cause the temperature of the oil to fall. Adjust the heat so that the oil is at least 180°C (350°F) when you lift the ingredients out. Oil drains off better at higher temperatures, so it's just as important to maintain the temperature at the end of each frying session as it is at the beginning.
4. Allow the oil to drain off properly immediately after frying. The best way is to put a few layers of kitchen paper (paper towel) on a tray or plate and allow the food to drain upright. Lean the pieces against each other for stability.

Karaage

からあげ

FRIED CHICKEN

Try to get boned chicken thighs with the skin on. This takes the fried-chicken experience to a completely different level!

SERVES 4

600g (1lb 5oz) boneless chicken thighs, preferably skin-on
vegetable oil, for deep frying
60g (½ cup) cornflour (cornstarch)
60g (½ cup) potato starch

FOR THE MARINADE
1 tsp finely grated garlic
1 tsp finely grated ginger
1½ tbsp Japanese soy sauce
1 tbsp mirin
1 tsp sake or dry white wine

TO SERVE
lemon wedges
mayonnaise
freshly boiled round-grain (sticky) rice (see page 47; optional)

PREPARATION

1. FOR THE MARINADE: Mix all the ingredients together in a bowl.
2. Cut the chicken thighs into bite-sized pieces and place in the marinade. Rub the marinade firmly into the meat with your hands. When the chicken is evenly coated, cover the bowl with a lid or cling film (plastic wrap) and leave in the fridge for at least 30 minutes.
3. Heat the oil in a large, deep pan to 190°C (375°F).
4. Mix the cornflour and potato starch in a large bowl or plastic bag. Place the chicken pieces in the mixture and make sure they are well coated with flour.
5. Fry the chicken in batches so the temperature of the oil doesn't fall too much. Fry for about 2–3 minutes until the pieces are light golden brown.
6. Leave to drain on kitchen paper (paper towel), then serve immediately. Serve hot with a few wedges of lemon for squeezing over, mayonnaise for dipping, and freshly boiled rice if serving as a main course.

Tonkatsu

とんかつ

PANKO-FRIED PORK

The Japanese version of schnitzel! Delicious eaten as it is, but it can also used in several other dishes. Here it's eaten like donburi, served on top of rice with shredded cabbage, and a tonkatsu sauce. Alternatively, it can served between white bread with a little mustard, mayonnaise, and sauce as in the Katsusando on page 81. This recipe uses pork, but you can make different katsu varieties – for example with beef, chicken, or fish.

SERVES 4

vegetable oil, for deep frying
4 slices of pork loin, about 2cm (¾in) thick, brought to room temperature for at least 30 minutes
2 tbsp plain (all-purpose) flour
2 tsp salt
1 tsp freshly ground black pepper
2–3 eggs, beaten
100g (2 cups) panko, ideally a mix of coarse and fine
hispi or any summer cabbage

FOR THE TONKATSU SAUCE (OR USE BANNOU SAUCE, SEE PAGE 13)

3½ tbsp ketchup
2 tbsp Japanese soy sauce
2 tbsp Worcestershire sauce
2 tbsp miso paste
2 tbsp sugar
2 tbsp hot water

TO SERVE

freshly boiled round-grain (sticky) rice (see page 47)
Japanese karashi mustard or Dijon mustard

PREPARATION

1. Combine the ingredients for the sauce and set aside.
2. Pour the oil into a saucepan or deep-fat fryer. If the loin slices are 2cm (¾in) thick, the oil should be at least 4cm (1½in) deep. Remove any tendons from the meat so the slices don't contract when fried.
3. Mix the flour, salt, and pepper in a plastic bag. Place one loin slice at a time in the bag, and shake until the meat is coated in the seasoned flour.
4. Remove each slice and dip first into the beaten egg and then the panko. Set aside on a tray.
5. Prepare the cabbage by slicing it thinly, ideally using a mandoline, and place it in iced water. Set aside.
6. Heat the oil to 190°C (375°F) and fry the loin slices for about 4 minutes until golden brown. Turn them now and then.
7. Keep an eye on the oil temperature to make sure it stays at about 180°C (350°F) during frying. If not, increase the heat. Leave the meat to drain on kitchen paper (paper towel).
8. Pour off the water from the cabbage and dry it in a salad spinner. Serve the tonkatsu with the sauce and cabbage, and ideally with freshly cooked rice and mustard on the side.

Katsusando

カツサンド

FRIED BEEF SANDWICH

Fry in the same way as for Tonkatsu on page 78. You can replace the beef with pork in this recipe if you like, but it works really well with steak.

SERVES 4

FOR THE KATSU
vegetable oil, for deep frying
2 tbsp plain (all-purpose) flour
2 tsp salt
1 tsp freshly ground black pepper
4 slices of beef or entrecôte, about 2cm (¾in) thick, fat trimmed off, brought to room temperature for at least 30 minutes
2–3 eggs, beaten
100g (2 cups) panko, ideally a mix of coarse and fine

FOR THE SANDO
8 slices of white bread
butter
240g (8½oz) hispi cabbage, finely shredded and placed in iced water
bannou Sauce (see page 13)
Japanese karashi mustard or Dijon mustard
mayonnaise

PREPARATION

1. Fry the meat in the same way as for Tonkatsu on page 78 (steps 2–4), and leave to drain.
2. Toast one side of the bread slices and smear a thin layer of butter on the untoasted sides.
3. Drain the cabbage really well and divide it between the buttered sides of four of the bread slices.
4. Spoon the bannou sauce over the katsu pieces, then place on top of the cabbage.
5. Spread a thin layer of mustard and then mayonnaise on the untoasted sides of the remaining 4 slices of bread.
6. Place these slices, mayonnaise-side down, on top of the katsu. Halve and serve.

Korokke

コロッケ

CROQUETTES

In Japan, many small shops that specialize in a specific foods – such as vegetables, fish, meat, or sweets – gather on the same street. In the meat shop there is often a small stand with a fryer where you can buy freshly fried croquettes. Japanese croquettes are made from potatoes mixed with meat and onions. I remember how my friends and I used to buy them on the way home from school to eat as a snack while they were still warm.

But why are the croquettes sold in the meat shop? Well, in Japan, you most often buy your meat in small pieces or thin slices. When the meat is cut up or sliced, there are always small pieces left over. Instead of throwing these away, they are mixed with potatoes and made into croquettes, as a way to make the most of the whole animal.

I use beef here, but you can also make a vegetarian version, replacing the meat with chopped mushrooms. If you can get hold of it, mix a coarse panko with a less coarse one for the coating.

You don't need sauce with these. Enjoy the potato flavour, the sweetness from the onions, the umami from the meat, and the wonderfully crispy crust.

SERVES 4 (16 CROQUETTES)

500g (1lb 2oz) potatoes, peeled and cut into 3cm (1¼in) pieces
120g (4¼oz) minced (ground) beef
420g (15oz) onion, finely chopped
1 tsp finely grated garlic
1 tbsp Japanese soy sauce
1 tsp salt
3 tbsp mirin
2 tbsp sake or white wine
1 tsp sugar
3½ tbsp water
vegetable oil, for deep frying
2 tbsp plain (all-purpose) flour
1 egg
3 tbsp full-fat milk
100g (2 cups) panko, ideally a mix of coarse and fine

PREPARATION

1. Place the potatoes, minced beef, onion, and garlic in a large saucepan with a lid. Add the soy sauce, salt, mirin, sake, sugar, and water.
2. Put the lid on and place the pan over a high heat. Wait until it begins to steam, then stir and reduce the heat to medium. Cook for about 20 minutes with the lid on.
3. Check whether the potatoes are soft. If not, cook for a few more minutes.
4. Remove the lid and increase the heat. Let the liquid almost boil away, then turn off the heat and mash the potatoes with a fork or potato masher.
5. Spread the mixture on a tray and leave to cool. Once cool, form into 16 croquettes.
6. Heat the oil to 190°C (375°F) in a saucepan or deep-fat fryer.
7. Meanwhile, mix the flour, egg, and milk in a large bowl and put the panko in another bowl.
8. Dip the croquettes first in the batter mixture and then in the panko, and fry them for 2 minutes until they have a nice golden colour and a crispy surface. Drain on kitchen paper (paper towels) and serve warm.

Tempura

天ぷら

FRIED VEGETABLES

My favourite seasonal ingredients are asparagus in spring; aubergine (eggplant), sweetcorn, and fresh spices in summer; mushrooms in autumn; and sweet potatoes in winter.

SERVES 4

2 bunches shimeji mushrooms
2 bunches enoki mushrooms
8 green asparagus spears
30g (1oz) coriander (cilantro)
vegetable oil, for deep frying

FOR THE TEMPURA BATTER
240ml (1 cup) ice-cold water
130g (1 cup) plain (all-purpose) flour, plus extra for dusting

FOR THE TEMPURA SAUCE
3½ tbsp dashi (see page 19), or use shop-bought
3½ tbsp Japanese soy sauce
2 tbsp mirin

TO SERVE
ponzu (see page 14), salt with matcha, or other seasonings

PREPARATION

1. Trim the mushrooms and divide into smaller bunches. Break off and discard the hard part of the asparagus stalks and peel about 10cm (4in) of the lower part. Trim the coriander and divide into 4 bouquets, using a stalk to tie them together.
2. Heat the oil to 190°C (375°F) in a saucepan or deep-fat fryer.
3. For the batter, pour the ice-cold water into a large bowl, add the flour, and whisk with a fork until the flour has sunk to the bottom. Stir (don't whisk, as gluten will form), with the back of the fork touching the bottom of the bowl, ten times. There should still be small lumps of flour in the batter.
4. Turn the vegetables in a little flour so they are coated in a thin layer, dip them in the batter, and then fry in the oil. They are ready when the surface is crispy and the air bubbles around the batter begin to get smaller. Drain on kitchen paper (paper towel). Mix the ingredients for the sauce.
5. Serve with the sauce and seasonings of your choice.

TOP TIP! Make sure the frying oil is at least 5cm (2in) deep, regardless of the size of the pan. Choose ingredients that don't contain too much liquid. For example, cucumber is not suitable for this method but fish, seafood, and meat are.

Sweetcorn kakiage

This is a variant of tempura where you cut the ingredients into smaller pieces (kaki) to fry (age).

MAKES ABOUT 20

2 fresh corn cobs
2 tbsp plain (all-purpose) flour
2 tbsp + 6½ tbsp tempura batter (see above)

1. Remove the sweetcorn kernels from the corn cobs and mix with the flour. Add the 2 tablespoons of tempura batter and stir until the mixture is sticky and coats the corn.
2. Add the remaining batter and mix lightly.
3. Carefully place spoonfuls of the mixture in the frying oil. Use a large spoon or paddle to shape them into balls. Fry until the surface is crispy, then drain on kitchen paper (paper towel) and serve with sauce and seasonings of your choice.

TOP TIP! When frying a small bundle of herb leaves or similar, first dip them in your batter, shake off lightly, then place the bundles of leaves in the frying oil and move them back and forth a little so that the leaves stay separate and aren't transformed into a single large clump.

Kushikatsu

串かつ

FRIED SKEWERS

Katsu means fried. Here is my recipe for kushikatsu – fried skewers. Thread whatever you like onto skewers, coat with panko, and deep fry.

SERVES 4

3 hispi cabbage leaves, blanched in salted water, then drained and dried
4 slices of bacon
8 small spring onions (scallions), trimmed and outer layer removed
8 small shiitake mushrooms, or 4 large ones, halved
1 small round Camembert, cut into 8 wedges
8 king prawns (jumbo shrimp)
90g (⅔ cup) plain (all-purpose) flour
1 large egg
100ml (scant ½ cup) water
100–150g (2–3 cups) panko
vegetable oil, for deep frying

TO SERVE

bannou Sauce (see page 13)
Japanese karashi mustard or Dijon mustard

PREPARATION

1. Place the cabbage leaves close together and lay the bacon slices on top. Roll up tightly and cut into 8 pieces. Thread 2 pieces onto each skewer.
2. Thread the spring onions, mushrooms, cheese, and prawns onto separate small skewers.
3. Mix the flour, egg, and water into a smooth batter and put the panko in a separate bowl. Dip the skewers in the batter, shake off any excess, and then roll in the panko. Be very careful to coat the cheese thoroughly.
4. Heat the oil to 180°C (350°F). Start by frying the spring onions, making sure the temperature stays at 180°C (350°F). When the spring onions start to colour, add the mushroom skewers, again maintaining the temperature of the oil. Once they are all golden brown, lift out onto kitchen paper (paper towel) to drain.
5. Increase the temperature of the oil to 185–190°C (365–375°F) and fry the cheese skewers. The temperature of the oil here is important so the cheese doesn't melt too much before it starts to brown. Drain as above.
6. Finally, fry the prawn and the cabbage and bacon skewers in batches and drain as above.
7. Serve with sauces and seasonings of your choice.

Fried & grilled

焼きもの

What do good fried dishes look like? Well, the surface of your chosen ingredient should be a nice golden brown and they are perfectly cooked and juicy inside. They look even more amazing when they have been brushed with a glaze and have a slightly charred and glossy finish.

To succeed with fried dishes, it's important that you carefully dry the surface of your ingredients before cooking. This makes all the difference, as a wet surface can ruin the frying process. It's also important to be patient and not to touch the ingredients in the pan until they have developed a good colour. Depending on which dish you're making, there are other things to consider too. With my top tips, I hope you'll be able to take fried dishes to new heights.

Shogayaki

生姜焼き

FRIED PORK IN GINGER SAUCE

This is one of the most popular home-cooked dishes in Japan. The delicious aroma of slightly charred soy sauce with ginger and garlic is mouth-watering. And the juicy fat from the pork makes it even more indulgent, even though it's an incredibly easy dish to make! You can eat classic shogayaki, with rice, salad, and perhaps miso soup, for both lunch and dinner.

The sauce also works very well with mackerel, so do try it out when mackerel is in season. Use whole fillets and fry them first skin-side down, then follow the steps in the recipe below, but cook the fish for another couple of minutes towards the end.

SERVES 4

600g (1lb 5oz) pork loin
2 tsp miso paste
4 tbsp Japanese soy sauce
4 tbsp mirin
1 tsp finely grated garlic
1 tbsp finely grated ginger
rapeseed (canola) oil, for frying
freshly ground black pepper
150g (5½oz) hispi cabbage, finely sliced
lettuce leaves
sliced tomato

1. Slice the pork loin as thinly as possible.
2. Mix the miso, soy sauce, mirin, garlic, and ginger in a bowl.
3. Heat a large frying pan with rapeseed oil over a high heat until it starts to smoke.
4. Place the meat slices in the pan, making sure they don't overlap. If you don't have a big enough pan, you can fry the meat in batches. Don't reduce the heat, but allow the meat to fry until it's nicely browned on one side – don't move or turn the slices – then lift them onto a plate and sprinkle with black pepper. The meat should only be half-cooked.
5. Using the same pan without washing it, add the soy mixture and turn the heat to high again. Allow to cook for 1 minute.
6. Return the meat to the pan, unfried-side down, and turn off the heat. The meat will be nicely cooked by the residual heat. (If necessary, adjust the time a little depending on how thin you managed to slice the meat. If it's a little thicker, you can turn on the heat for a minute or so to be sure the meat is cooked through.)
7. Place the finely sliced hispi cabbage, lettuce leaves and tomato slices on a plate and top with the meat. Pour over a few spoonfuls of the sauce to finish, and serve with freshly boiled rice (see page 47) if you like.

Gyoza

餃子

FRIED DUMPLINGS

When I'm in Japan on hot summer days and see a sign that says gyoza, I immediately want to go in and order gyoza with a beer, which is often served in an ice-cold glass. Here I include my favourite filling of prawns; choose one of the fillings – or make a batch of each!

SERVES 4 (MAKES ABOUT 50 GYOZA)
about 50 gyoza wrappers
rapeseed (canola) oil, for frying

OPTION 1: PRAWN FILLING
300g (10½oz) king prawns (jumbo shrimp)
15g (½oz) spring onions (scallions), white parts only, finely chopped
30g (1oz) hispi cabbage, finely chopped
20g (¾oz) celery, finely chopped
½ tbsp finely grated garlic
½ tbsp finely grated ginger
1 tsp sesame oil
1 tsp salt
freshly ground black pepper

OPTION 2: MEAT FILLING
200g (7oz) mixed minced (ground) beef and pork, or minced (ground) chicken
½ tbsp finely grated garlic
½ tbsp finely grated ginger
15g (½oz) spring onions (scallions), white parts only, finely chopped
30g (1oz) hispi cabbage, finely chopped
20g (¾oz) celery, finely chopped
1 tsp sesame oil
1 tsp salt
2 tbsp water
freshly ground black pepper

SERVING OPTIONS
50/50 Japanese soy sauce and rice vinegar
ponzu (see page 14)
taberu rayu (see page 14) or yuzu kosho
rice vinegar with freshly ground black pepper

1. FOR THE PRAWN FILLING: Clean the prawns and remove the dark vein. Cut six of the prawns into 4 pieces each and mix or chop the rest into a fine paste. Mix the prawns with the spring onions, hispi cabbage, celery, garlic, ginger, sesame oil, salt, and pepper.
2. FOR THE MEAT FILLING: Knead the minced meat in a large bowl until it releases some fat and develops an airy texture. Add 1 tablespoon of rapeseed oil and the remaining ingredients and mix.
3. Fold your chosen mixture into the gyoza wrappers (see the step-by-step images on the next page).
4. Heat some rapeseed oil in a pan (with a lid) over a medium heat. When the oil has almost started to smoke, place the gyoza close together in the pan and fry until the bottom of each dumpling is light brown. Pour in 3½ tablespoons of water and cover. Fry for another 1 minute without opening the lid.
5. Remove the lid and fry for about 1 minute until the gyoza develop a deeper colour on the bottom and start to loosen from the pan. Drizzle 1 tablespoon of rapeseed oil around the edge of the pan. Place a large plate over the frying pan and turn upside down so that the gyoza end up on the plate fried-side up.
6. Serve with your choice of dipping sauces.

Shake teriyaki

鮭の照り焼き

TERIYAKI SALMON

Teriyaki is a well-known dish to anyone who loves Japanese food. The word means glossy (teri) and fried/grilled (yaki), and usually involves brushing meat or fish with sauce while on the grill, so the food takes on the aroma of the lightly caramelized sauce. As the sauce is reduced on the surface of the food, it creates a nicely glossy finish and the flavours become even more concentrated. In lots of places, chicken teriyaki is most often found on the menu, but you can also cook different types of meat and fish (or vegetables) this way. Here's a simple version with salmon that can be cooked in a frying pan.

SERVES 4

1 tbsp rapeseed (canola) oil
2 garlic cloves, halved lengthways
about 500g (1lb 2oz) salmon fillet, cut into 4 pieces
3 tbsp tare (see page 13)

TO SERVE
mayonnaise
tomato wedges
lettuce or Chinese cabbage
freshly boiled round-grain (sticky) rice (see page 47)

PREPARATION

1. Add the rapeseed oil and garlic cloves to a frying pan (with a lid) and place over a medium heat. When the oil begins to smoke, turn the garlic halves over and add the salmon fillets, skin-side down.
2. Fry the fillets for about 2 minutes, with the lid on, until they develop a nice sear. Turn the salmon over, put on the lid, and fry for a further 1–3 minutes depending on the thickness of the fish. Make sure the garlic doesn't burn – lift it out when it is golden brown and, if you like, set it aside for serving.
3. Tilt the pan and soak up the oil with kitchen paper (paper towel). Pour in the tare, swirl it around the pan and spoon the sauce onto the salmon for 30 seconds while frying.
4. Serve immediately with mayonnaise, tomato wedges, lettuce, or Chinese cabbage, and freshly boiled rice on the side.

Yakitori

焼き鳥

CHICKEN SKEWERS

My favourite smell is when the fat from the chicken and glaze drips onto charcoal in a slightly shabby and smoky yakitori place. I have a memory of this kind of small place, run by a man who barbecued the food while his mother served it. Almost everyone there seemed to be regulars. When I left, I called to the cook: "Thanks! That was the best yakitori I've ever eaten!" And all the regulars at the bar turned and looked at me with broad smiles. They looked so proud, and one of them shouted: "See you again soon!" Memories like this make me feel warm inside – and so eager to eat yakitori that I stand in our courtyard grilling food even in the winter.

Yakitori is a Japanese version of chicken skewers. In restaurants, there are usually many different parts of the chicken on the menu – from breast and thighs to offal. Here I have used parts that are quite easy to get hold of. You can choose to make one or more versions of the skewers.

You can also choose between shio (salt) or tare (glaze) to eat them with. When served with tare, they're like a kind of teriyaki (see page 102). You can cook yakitori in a frying pan, but if you're able to grill over charcoal or birch wood, I think you should!

SERVES 4

NEGIMA (CHICKEN & SPRING ONIONS)
500g (1lb 2oz) skin-on chicken thighs, cut into bite-sized pieces
5 spring onions (scallions), cut into 2cm (¾in) pieces

KIMO & HATSU (LIVER & HEART)
300g (10½oz) chicken liver and/or heart

TSUKUNE (MEATBALLS)
70g (2½oz) shiitake or chestnut (cremini) mushrooms, shredded
1 tsp sesame oil
2 tsp rapeseed (canola) oil
200g (7oz) minced (ground) chicken
⅓ tsp salt
1 egg white
1 tsp finely grated garlic
1 tsp finely grated ginger
30g (1oz) onion, finely chopped

FOR GRILLING
wooden skewers
tare (see page 13)
salt (for yakitori shio, see step 6 overleaf)

TO SERVE (OPTIONAL)
shichimi togarashi
yuzu kosho
freshly ground black pepper

PREPARATION

1. Soak your skewers in water before use, preferably for a few hours.
2. FOR THE TSUKUNE: Mix the mushrooms, sesame oil, and rapeseed oil in a bowl. Knead the chicken mince and salt in another bowl until it starts to become a sticky batter. Mix well with the egg white, mushrooms, garlic, ginger, and onion. Leave the mixture to rest for at least 1 hour in the fridge. Mould into egg shapes or make small pancakes and then grill (or fry in a pan). If you want, you can brush with tare at the end of the grilling process.
3. FOR THE NEGIMA: Thread the chicken and spring onions onto skewers and have some skewers with only chicken.
4. FOR THE KIMO & HATSU: Trim any tendons from the liver and/or heart and cut into bite-sized pieces. If the pieces are small to start with, you can leave whole and make a few cuts in the surface. Place in iced water (separately if using both liver and heart) and change the water a few times until it runs clear. Lift out and dry on kitchen paper (paper towel), then thread the pieces onto your skewers.
5. Grill your meats (placing chicken thighs skin-side down first). Once the undersides have developed a nice colour, brush the surface of the meat with tare and turn over. When the tare begins to char slightly, brush the meat and turn over again, repeating several times until the meats are cooked.
6. If you want to make yakitori shio, grill without tare and instead brush with a little rapeseed oil and finish with salt.

TOP TIP! Onigiri (see page 69) work very well when grilled with tare. Start by brushing the surface with oil, then grill/fry until they develop a nice colour. Brush with tare and continue grilling, making sure that the brushed side is down after each brushing, otherwise the rice grains will separate.

Okonomiyaki

お好み焼き

HEARTY CABBAGE PANCAKES

Okonomiyaki are often called Japanese pancakes. When I was studying in Nishinomiya my favourite place to eat them was restaurant called Michi, close to where I lived. It was a small restaurant with an L-shaped table where the guests sat in a row on the outside of the L, and on the inside a woman cooked okonomiyaki for the patrons. Her voice was memorably loud and high-pitched, and she always had a huge smile. When you came in, she would shout "Welcome!", and when you left, "Thank you very much! See you again soon!" Her okonomiyaki were the best in town and I was sad to learn that the restaurant had permanently closed in 2020. It was a tiny place with eight seats, but I will never forget it.

You will find different varieties of okonomiyaki depending on where you are in Japan. Here is my version, inspired by the versions from Osaka and Hiroshima.

Osaka-style

In Osaka, okonomiyaki are made with lots of cabbage, spring onions, and pickled ginger in the batter, and fried with pork or any protein.

SERVES 4

260g (2 cups) plain (all-purpose) flour
3 eggs
250ml (1 cup) dashi (see page 19), or use shop-bought
300g (10½oz) hispi cabbage, finely chopped
60g (2oz) spring onions (scallions), finely sliced
2 tbsp gari (pickled ginger), finely chopped
rapeseed (canola) oil, for frying

TOPPING
100g (3½oz) pork belly, cut into slices 1–2mm (¹⁄₁₆in) thick, or prawns (shrimp) or octopus

TO SERVE
katsuobushi
mayonnaise
aonori (seaweed powder)
bannou sauce (see page 13)

PREPARATION

1. Whisk together the flour, eggs, and dashi in a large bowl until smooth.
2. Add the cabbage, spring onions, and pickled ginger, and mix the batter with a spatula.
3. Heat 1 tablespoon of rapeseed oil in a 22cm (8½in) frying pan (with a lid) over a medium heat until it starts to smoke. Add one quarter of your topping of choice and then immediately one quarter of the batter. Spread it out so the batter coats the whole bottom of the pan and fry for 3 minutes, covered, until golden brown.
4. Turn the pancake gently, replace the lid and fry for another 3 minutes.
5. Turn the pancake again, drip another tablespoon of oil around the edge of the pan and fry for another 3 minutes without the lid until it is done.
6. Place the okonomiyaki on a plate with the topping side up.
7. Top with katsuobushi, mayonnaise, aonori, and bannou sauce to serve. Make the other 3 pancakes in the same way.

Hiroshima yaki

In the area around Hiroshima, the batter is fried in very thin pancakes before cabbage, onion, protein, eggs and noodles are piled on top.

SERVES 4

130g (1 cup) plain (all-purpose) flour
200ml (scant 1 cup) dashi (see page 19), or use shop-bought, or water
rapeseed (canola) oil, for frying
200g (7oz) shredded cabbage
200g (7oz) beansprouts
100g (3½oz) pork belly, cut into slices 1–2mm (¹⁄₁₆in) thick, or prawns (shrimp) or octopus
100g (3½oz) cooked egg noodles
4 eggs

TO SERVE

bannou sauce (see page 13)
mayonnaise
aonori (seaweed powder)
katsuobushi

PREPARATION

1. Mix the flour and dashi in a large bowl.
2. Heat a 22cm (8½in) frying pan over a medium heat. Pour in a little rapeseed oil and swirl it around the pan. Pour in 60ml (¼ cup) of the batter and tilt the pan to distribute the batter evenly. Place a quarter of the cabbage and a quarter of the beansprouts on top of the batter, then add a quarter of the pork (or prawns or octopus). Spoon a little more batter over the top (so you've used a quarter of the batter in total) and fry for a few minutes until the bottom of the pancake has developed a touch of colour. Flip using two spatulas and continue frying so that the pork, cabbage, and beansprouts cook underneath the pancake "lid".
3. When the pancake is just cooked, heat a separate pan over a high heat, pour in some oil, and fry a quarter of the noodles. When the noodles are warmed through, carefully lift up the cabbage pancake and place it on top of the noodles. Reduce the heat to low.
4. Place the first pan over a high heat with a little rapeseed oil. When it starts to smoke, crack in one of the eggs and turn off the heat. Shape the egg pancake into a round, stir lightly, then carefully lift the cooked cabbage and noodle pancake from the second pan and place it on top of the egg layer.
5. Brush with bannou sauce and drizzle with mayonnaise, then sprinkle with aonori and katsuobushi to serve. Make the other 3 pancakes in the same way.

Stews & soups

鍋もの汁もの

Japanese stews are often cooked for less time than Western ones, and take into account the flavour and consistency of the different ingredients. These stews are even tastier the next day, which is often the case with such dishes. Given their short preparation time, they can work well even as a weekday meal. This chapter also includes *à la minute* stews and miso soup.

Sukiyaki

すき焼き

STEW WITH MEAT & VEGETABLES

Every New Year's Eve until I turned 16, my father's family gathered around a large table bearing two saucepans on a portable gas stove and ate sukiyaki until my brothers and cousins and I were very full and the adults were tipsy and happy. I enjoyed sukiyaki, and my family ate it from time to time, but the sukiyaki on New Year's Eve was always special for me. I got to be with cousins I didn't see very often because they lived in another part of Japan. It also brought the feeling that another year had passed and expectations of the big New Year's Day celebration the next day. I felt the pride of completing another year, and hope for the new one to come. It's a very vivid food memory, and I get nostalgic every time I eat sukiyaki.

SERVES 4

12 shiitake mushrooms
2 bunches enoki mushrooms
1 leek
¼ Chinese cabbage
200g (7oz) firm or silken tofu
rapeseed (canola) oil, for frying
600g (1lb 5oz) beef or entrecôte, thinly sliced
4 eggs
2 portions cooked udon noodles (optional)

FOR THE SAUCE
200ml (scant 1 cup) Japanese soy sauce
200ml (scant 1 cup) mirin
200ml (scant 1 cup) sake or dry white wine
1 tbsp sugar

PREPARATION

1. FOR THE SAUCE: Mix all the ingredients together and set aside.
2. PREPARE THE VEGETABLES: Remove the stem from the shiitake and cut a cross in the surface of the caps. Trim off the base of the enoki mushrooms and divide them into smaller bundles. Cut the leek into diagonal slices about 1.5cm (¾in) thick. Pick off the Chinese cabbage leaves one by one, halve lengthways and cut into 4cm (1½in)-long pieces. Cut the tofu into bite-sized pieces (if using firm tofu, enhance the flavour by frying it on all sides first until it develops a little colour).
3. Heat a saucepan (with a lid) over a high heat, pour in a little oil, and add as many slices of beef as will fit, so that the bottom is covered without the pieces overlapping each other. Pour in half of the sauce and allow to glaze. Remove the meat from the pan and set aside.
4. Reduce the heat to medium and add a few pieces of each vegetable (except the enoki) and a few pieces of tofu to the pan. Pour in 200ml (scant 1 cup) of the sauce and simmer for 3–5 minutes, with the lid on, until the vegetables are cooked.
5. Remove the lid, return the meat to the pan and add the enoki. Simmer for a further 1 minute before inviting everyone to start eating, by picking out ingredients from the pan, which they then eat from their own bowls. Allow the stew to continue simmering over a low heat while you eat.
6. Meanwhile, crack the eggs into separate dipping bowls, whisk, then dip the meat and vegetables into the raw eggs. Continue adding ingredients and sauce to the pan and allow them to cook while you eat, like a hot pot.
7. When all the ingredients are finished, you can put the udon noodles in the pan to mop up the last of the sauce.

Shabu shabu

しゃぶしゃぶ

JAPANESE HOT POT

The broth for this dish can be flavoured in different ways, and there are variants with everything from soya milk to kimchi. Here I have made the simplest one, which is called mizutaki. You start by heating water containing just a sheet of kombu, and as the different ingredients are added to (and cooked in) the broth, it develops a fantastic flavour.

The meal ends by adding boiled rice or noodles to soak up the last of the broth. The name shabu shabu comes from the sound of dipping finely cut meat into the warm broth and shaking it twice – a clever way to get perfectly cooked meat.

SERVES 4–6

2 litres (8½ cups) water
10cm (4in) kombu
600g (1lb 5oz) beef or entrecôte, thinly sliced
1 leek, cut on the diagonal into 1cm (½in)-thick slices
150g (5½oz) shiitake, stems removed and a couple of incisions cut into each cap
300g (10½oz) firm or silken tofu, cut into bite-sized pieces
150g (5½oz) oyster mushrooms
¼ head Chinese cabbage, halved and cut into 5cm (2in) pieces
50g (1¾oz) fresh spinach

FOR THE RICE PORRIDGE
1 bowl of cooked round-grain (sticky) rice (see page 47)
2 eggs, lightly beaten
3 spring onions (scallions), finely sliced

TO SERVE
gomadare (see page 15)
ponzu (see page 14)
yuzu kosho
shichimi togarashi

PREPARATION

1. Prepare all the ingredients and arrange them attractively on a plate. Set out individual small sauce bowls.
2. Boil the water and kombu in a large pot, preferably on a gas stove in the middle of the table, then reduce the heat until the broth is simmering.
3. Cook the ingredients by adding them to the pot in batches and allowing everyone to remove and eat what they want. Gradually top up the pot with more ingredients.
4. FOR THE RICE PORRIDGE: When all the ingredients have been eaten, add the rice to the remaining broth. Simmer for about 1 minute, then drizzle over the lightly beaten eggs and simmer for another minute with the lid on. Sprinkle with the spring onions and eat as the conclusion to the meal.

There are many variations of the hot pot in Japan, but all of them involve sitting together around a table with a pot bubbling away in the middle, from which different ingredients are selected and dipped in tasty sauces.

Kare-raisu

カレーライス

JAPANESE CURRY

When India was occupied by the British, the British took curry home and developed their own version. This "English" curry later came to Japan, where it developed into what is now kare-raisu ("curry rice" in Japanese). There are recipes for how to mix your own spices, but most Japanese households simply buy ready-made curry cubes. The flavour and heat can vary slightly depending on the brand of curry paste, so experiment until you find the strength you want.

SERVES 4

2 tbsp rapeseed (canola) oil
450g (1lb) braising steak, cut into slices 0.5–1cm (¼–½in) thick, and each slice divided into 2 pieces
450g (1lb) onions, half finely sliced and half cut into 3cm (1¼in)-thick wedges
1 large garlic clove, finely grated
1 tbsp sugar
3 tbsp rice vinegar or white or red wine vinegar
180g (6¼oz) carrots, peeled and cut into 3cm (1¼in) pieces
200g (7oz) potatoes, peeled and cut into 1cm (½in) pieces
100ml (scant ½ cup) + 800ml (generous 3½ cups) water
110g (3¾oz) Japanese curry paste cubes
salt and freshly ground black pepper

TO SERVE

freshly boiled round-grain (sticky) rice (see page 47)
rakkyo (pickled Japanese shallots) or pickled onions (optional)
fukujinzuke (dried and pickled radish); optional

PREPARATION

1. Heat the rapeseed oil in a saucepan (with a lid) over a high heat and, once hot, fry the slices of beef in batches. Season lightly with salt and pepper, then remove the beef from the pan and set aside.
2. Place the finely sliced onions, garlic, sugar, and rice vinegar in the same saucepan without washing it out. Increase the heat and cook with the lid on for 1 minute, then stir, making sure you scrape the bottom of the pan. Repeat the process until the onions are lightly caramelized.
3. Add the onion wedges, carrots, potatoes, and meat to the pan, along with the 100ml (scant ½ cup) water. Stir and fry over a medium heat, with the lid on. Stir at regular intervals, until the potatoes and carrots are soft at the edges.
4. Add the 800ml (generous 3½ cups) water and place over a high heat. Skim if you like, but this isn't necessary. As soon as it comes to the boil, reduce to a medium-low heat and leave to simmer with the lid on until the carrots and potatoes are completely soft.
5. Remove the lid, add the curry paste cubes and allow to melt into the sauce.
6. Serve with freshly cooked rice, and pickled onions and/or radish if you like.

Sūpu

スープ

SOUP

Soup made from good dashi warms your stomach and is something you don't want to miss in a Japanese meal. Most vegetables work in soup, but why not use those that are in season? I love miso soup made from fresh cabbage with its soft early-spring leaves. Here are two versions with miso and one without, where you get a more immediate flavour of dashi.

Miso with potatoes & onions

SERVES 4

600ml (generous 2½ cups) dashi (see page 19), or use shop-bought
2 potatoes, peeled and cut into slices about 3mm (⅛in) thick
1 onion, cut into thin wedges
4 tsp miso paste

PREPARATION

1. Place the dashi, potatoes, and onions in a saucepan and bring to the boil. Reduce the heat and simmer until the potatoes are cooked through.
2. Pass the miso paste through a sieve and add to the soup (or put the miso paste in a bowl, dilute with a little dashi and stir, then add back to the soup).
3. Turn off the heat so that it doesn't reduce and get too salty.

Miso with fresh cabbage

SERVES 4

600ml (generous 2½ cups) dashi (see page 19), or use shop-bought
200g (7oz) fresh cabbage or hispi cabbage, leaves shredded into 1cm (½in)-wide strips and stalk finely sliced on an angle
4 tsp miso paste
shichimi togarashi

PREPARATION

1. Bring the dashi and the stalk of the cabbage to the boil in a saucepan. Once the broth is boiling, add the leaves and simmer for 1 minute. Turn off the heat.
2. Pass the miso paste through a sieve and add to the soup. Serve sprinkled with shichimi togarashi.

Dashi with eggs

SERVES 4

600ml (generous 2½ cups) dashi (see page 19), or use shop-bought
1 tbsp fish sauce
1 tsp Japanese soy sauce
2 eggs
1 tsp sesame oil
salt and freshly ground black pepper

PREPARATION

1. Place the dashi, fish sauce, soy sauce, and a little salt in a saucepan and bring to the boil, then reduce the heat and allow to simmer.
2. Whisk the eggs and 2 pinches of salt in a bowl. Drizzle this into the soup in a thin stream, using chopsticks to create fluffy streamers as you pour. Continue to simmer for 1 minute, then add the sesame oil.
3. Pour the soup into bowls and grind over some black pepper to serve.

130

Small plates

小皿料理

In Japanese cuisine, we eat many small dishes with rice. This is a great way to get different forms of protein and nutrition in a meal, and it also makes for a very colourful dining table. Here are some simple and quick dishes that can be made at the last moment to add a nice touch to any meal. I also give you a little inspiration for how to make a bento – a Japanese lunch box – which could consist of a collection of small dishes from the previous day's dinner...

Sashimi

刺身

RAW FISH

A unique feature of Japanese food culture is that you eat raw fish – sashimi. It's not easy to get hold of as many different types of fish in Western supermarkets, but you can still try it out when you find good-quality fish that suits being served as sashimi. Here are a few different techniques for preparing the fish.

MAKES ABOUT 70G (2½OZ) PER PERSON

salmon
tuna (plus a marinade of equal parts Japanese soy sauce and mirin)
turbot (plus a sheet of kombu)
scallops

TO SERVE
wasabi
Japanese soy sauce
ponzu (see page 14)
salt
shiso or lettuce leaves

PREPARATION

1. SALMON: Cut into 2mm (1/16in)-thick slices.
2. TUNA: Cut into 1.5cm (¾in)-thick, rectangular pieces. Blanch for 2 seconds in boiling water and then plunge into iced water for 5 seconds. Dry thoroughly and briefly place in a marinade of equal parts Japanese soy sauce and mirin.
3. TURBOT: Buy or cut out a fillet and remove the skin. Cut into thin slices, making them as flat and with as large a surface area as possible by angling the knife blade. Quickly dip your sheet of kombu in a bowl of cold water to soften it slightly, then pat dry and neatly place the slices of turbot on the kombu to "cure" for 10 minutes.
4. SCALLOPS: Open each scallop by scraping with a knife inside the shell of the flat part. Remove the lid and release the scallop meat using a spoon in the round side of the shell. Remove the membranes and wipe the scallop with kitchen paper (paper towel). Cut each scallop meat in half.
5. Place the fish you prepared for your sashimi on a plate, preferably on a layer of ice. Serve with your choice of accompaniments, such as wasabi, soy sauce, ponzu, salt, and shiso and/or lettuce leaves.

Tsukemono

漬物

PICKLES

Tsukemono are preserved vegetables – usually by pickling – and they come in many different styles. One technique is to simply rub salt into the vegetables to quickly draw out their liquid. Another is to add herbs or spices and allow the vegetable to release its liquid, which it is then pickled in. It's called fruzuke when something is pickled for a little longer, and asazuke when something is pickled quickly.

You decide when your pickles are ready – if you allow the vegetables to stand for a little longer, they begin to undergo lactic fermentation, which gives a slight, delightful acidity, and umami flavour.

There are many different seasonings to choose from. For example, try adding shredded shiso leaves, sage, basil, cumin, or sansho pepper. Here are five simple, delicious recipes.

Pickled radish

250g (9oz) radishes without the leaves (keep the leaves if nice and fresh)
1½ tsp salt
1 tsp sugar
1 tsp rice vinegar

PREPARATION

1. Place the radishes in a jar or bowl with a lid. Sprinkle with the salt and sugar and pour over the vinegar, then stir or shake with the lid on. Leave to stand for at least 1 hour or a maximum of overnight at room temperature. Turn the jar from time to time so the released liquid washes over the radishes. Eat immediately or store in the fridge for up to 7 days.

Pickled cucumber

1 cucumber (about 270g/9½oz)
⅓ tsp salt
1 tsp mirin
1 tsp rice vinegar
6g (⅛oz) kombu, broken into small pieces

PREPARATION

1. Quarter the cucumber lengthways and deseed. Cut into bite-sized pieces and mix with the salt, mirin, and kombu. Stir and leave to stand for about 15 minutes at room temperature.
2. Stir again and leave to stand for another 15 minutes at room temperature.
3. Eat immediately or cover and store in the fridge for up to 5 days. I always think the cucumber is best on the second day.

Pickled celery

250g (9oz) celery
1 tsp salt
1 tsp rice vinegar
1 tsp sesame oil

PREPARATION
1. Peel the celery and cut it into bite-sized pieces. Rub with the salt, vinegar, and sesame oil. Pack the celery tightly in a jar or bowl and leave for about 30 minutes at room temperature. Turn a few times. Eat immediately as crispy asazuke or cover and store for up to 3 days in the fridge.

Pickled carrot

250g (9oz) carrots
2 tbsp miso paste
2 tbsp mirin

PREPARATION
1. Peel the carrots and halve them lengthways if they are thick. Mix the miso and mirin together, and rub the mixture into the carrots. Pack the carrots tightly in a jar or bowl and leave for about 30 minutes at room temperature, turning a few times. Wipe the miso mixture off with kitchen paper (paper towel) and cut the carrots into bite-sized pieces to serve. Eat immediately as crispy asazuke or cover and store for up to 7 days in the fridge.

Pickled Chinese cabbage with chilli

250g (9oz) Chinese cabbage
1½ tsp salt
a few slices of dried chilli

PREPARATION
1. Separate the Chinese cabbage leaves and halve them lengthways. Rub the salt and chilli into the leaves and then leave to stand for about 30 minutes at room temperature, or at most overnight. Cover and store in the fridge for about 7 days. When serving, squeeze out the liquid thoroughly and cut the leaves into pieces.

Dashimaki tamago

だし巻き卵

JAPANESE OMELETTE

You need a special rectangular pan to make a Japanese omelette. You can also make one in a normal round frying pan, although it won't be as neat.

MAKES 4 SMALL PORTIONS

3 eggs
3½ tbsp dashi (see page 19), or use shop-bought
2 pinches of salt
1½ tsp mirin
2 tbsp rapeseed (canola) oil
1 tsp sesame oil

PREPARATION

1. Mix the eggs, dashi, salt, and mirin in a large bowl.
2. Mix the rapeseed oil and sesame oil on a small plate. Fold a small piece of kitchen paper (paper towel) into a square and use it to brush oil onto the pan during cooking.
3. Heat your omelette pan or a frying pan over a medium heat. When the pan is hot, brush it with oil, using the kitchen paper. Pour in about one-fifth of the batter.
4. Wait for a short while, until the batter bubbles, then stir a little and make a "core" by folding/rolling the egg towards you (see the photos over the page).
5. Slide the omelette to the back edge of the pan and pour in another one-fifth of the batter. Lift the core a little and allow the fresh batter to spread evenly across the pan.
6. When the batter bubbles, once again fold the core towards you, rolling up the new layer with it, then push it to the back edge of the pan again. Be careful and as quick as possible to make sure it doesn't colour too much.
7. Repeat the process until you have used up all the batter.
8. When the roll is finished, place the tamago on a sushi mat or clean tea (dish) towel and neaten the shape a little.
9. Cut into pieces and serve immediately, preferably with grated radish flavoured with a little soy sauce.

Hiyayakko

冷奴

COLD TOFU DISHES

These are perfect, quick small dishes or accompaniments to a meal. On hot summer days I usually make one of these dishes with a whole packet of silken tofu and eat it as a main course.

Hiyayakko with katsuobushi

MAKES 4 SMALL PORTIONS

½ packet silken tofu
5g (⅙oz) katsuobushi
Japanese soy sauce or ponzu (see page 14)

Place the silken tofu on a plate. Top with katsuobushi and drizzle with soy sauce or ponzu.

Hiyayakko with salmon roe

MAKES 4 SMALL PORTIONS

½ packet silken tofu
80g (2¾oz) salmon or trout roe
Japanese soy sauce

Place the silken tofu on a plate. Top with the salmon or trout roe and drizzle with soy sauce.

Hiyayakko with sesame oil

MAKES 4 SMALL PORTIONS

½ packet silken tofu
1 tbsp finely grated ginger
2 spring onions (scallions), green parts only, finely sliced
sesame oil
flaky salt

Place the silken tofu on a plate. Top with the ginger and spring onions, then drizzle with sesame oil and sprinkle with a little flaky salt.

Bento

冷奴

LUNCH BOX

Bento is usually translated as lunch box. In Japan, it is quite common to bring a bento box to school or work every day. Some people cook all the components of their bento from scratch every morning, while others use the leftovers from yesterday's dinner or a combination of the two.

When I went to school I got school lunches, so I only took bento with me on outings or for sports day – it always felt like such a treat. My favourite combination was karaage (which goes soft from the moisture in the box), onigiri with umeboshi, toasted sesame seeds and salmon, and tamagoyaki (omelette).

My mother was very good at making colourful bento boxes, but I do remember one particularly disappointing bento that she made for me when I was a teenager. When I opened the box at lunchtime, I was expecting to see the familiar flash of colour. Instead, I saw that the first row was filled with rice and the second with brown yakisoba! I had to close the lid embarrassed so that my friends, who all had colourful lunches, wouldn't see. It was delicious however, and I laugh now when I think back to it.

KEY TIPS

1. Wipe/dab any excess moisture from the surface of your food and the inside of your bento box.
2. Season your food a little less, as the flavours are stronger when food is cold.
3. Add colours such as yellow, red, and green – both because it looks good and it's more nutritious.
4. Pack everything tightly so it doesn't move around when you're carrying the box.
5. For the bento box in the photograph, I have used gyudon (see page 56) – the sauce from the beef seeps into the rice, keeping it soft and juicy; tsukemono (pickles; see page 135), which add a touch of freshness and contain little liquid so won't make the rest of the box soggy; and tamagoyaki, for its comforting yellow colour. And then as a finishing touch, I've included green beans with gomadare sauce, and aubergine (eggplant) with taberu rayu (see page 16). I hope this gives you a little inspiration for your own lunch box!

Pafe

冷奴

PARFAIT

There are many sweet dishes from Japan. Pafe is one of the most popular Western-inspired desserts, and people sometimes queue for hours to buy it from the best places. When I was small, I loved chocolate-flavoured pafe and I loved that my dad allowed me to eat it when we were together. This is an adult version with Japanese flavours. The recipe is intended to make a small dessert for after a meal, but if you want more you can just double the recipe.

SERVES 4

300g (1¼ cups) vanilla ice cream
12 strawberries, quartered
5 tsp matcha powder, sifted
100ml (scant ½ cup) lukewarm water

FOR THE CRUMBS
8 digestive biscuits (graham crackers), finely crushed
3 tbsp kinako (roasted soya flour)
40g (1½oz) butter

FOR THE SAUCE
90g (scant ½ cup) muscovado sugar
3½ tbsp water
2 pinches of salt

PREPARATION

1. FOR THE CRUMBS: Place the digestives and kinako in a large bowl. Brown the butter in a small saucepan and pour it into the bowl. Mix thoroughly and leave to cool.
2. FOR THE SAUCE: Bring the ingredients to the boil in a saucepan, simmer for 1 minute, and leave to cool.
3. Layer up the ice cream, strawberries, sauce, and crumbs in 4 tall/sundae glasses.
4. Place the matcha in a bowl, drizzle over the water, and whisk thoroughly, preferably with a matcha whisk or ordinary hand whisk. Pour over the ice cream and serve.

A Japanese meal

一汁三菜

A Japanese meal is structured according to the concept of ichijuu sansai – a soup and three dishes that are served in different bowls or on plates. There is usually a soup, a main course (generally a protein such as meat or fish), and two smaller dishes containing vegetables and rice, with tsukemono (pickles; see page 135) on the side. By adopting this tried-and-tested philosophy, you will find it easier to eat in a more balanced and healthy way.

But on a normal weekday it may not be so straightforward to prepare several different dishes, using lots of pots and pans. The recipes in this book are designed with the hope that you will have the energy to make them even on weekdays. I think all of the recipes work very well served on a plate with rice as a main course, or served alongside several dishes to share in the izakaya (Japanese pub) style.

Donburi (bowl)

Urushi-wan (lacquer bowl)

Urushi donburi (large lacquer bowl)

Shiru-wan (soup bowl)

Kodomo-chawan (rice bowl for children)

Futamono (bowl with lid)

Kobachi (small bowl)

Chawan (rice bowl)

Mame zara (small plate)

Mori zara (plate)

Urushi zara (lacquer plate)

Garasu zara (glass plate)

Gurasu (glass)

Shoyu sashi (soy sauce jug)

Suihan nabe (rice cooker)

Bentobako (wooden lunch box)

Index

aonori 11
   onkonomiyaki (hearty cabbage pancakes) 111–12
   yakisoba 42
apples/apple juice, bannou sauce 13
arare, shake ikura chazuke (rice in tea with salmon & salmon roe) 65
asparagus, tempura 87–88
aubergines, deep fried 16

bacon
   kushikatsu (fried skewers) 90
   yakisoba 42
bannou sauce 13
   katsusando 81
   onkonomiyaki (hearty cabbage pancakes) 111–12
   yakisoba 42
beansprouts
   hiyashichuka (summer noodles) 41
   onkonomiyaki (hearty cabbage pancakes) 112
   otsumami (quick dishes) 16
   shoyu ramen 29
beef
   gyoza 99
   gyudon (rice with beef) 56
   kare-raisu (Japanese curry) 127
   katsusando 81
   korokke (croquettes) 83
   shabu shabu (Japanese hot pot) 121
   sukiyaki (stew with meat & vegetables) 118
   beni shoga 10
   gyudon (rice with beef) 56
   yakisoba 42
bento 144
biscuits, pafe (parfait) 146
bowls, plates and other containers 149
bread, katsusando 81

cabbage
   gyoza 99
   katsusando 81
   kushikatsu (fried skewers) 90
   miso soup with fresh cabbage 128
   miso with fresh cabbage 128
   onkonomiyaki (hearty cabbage pancakes) 111–12
   pickled Chinese cabbage with chilli 136
   shabu shabu (Japanese hot pot) 121
   shogayaki (fried pork in ginger sauce) 96
   sukiyaki (stew with meat & vegetables) 118
   tonkatsu 78
   yakisoba 42
carrots
   kare-raisu (Japanese curry) 127
   omuraisu (omelette & rice) 49–50
   pickled carrot 136
   yakisoba 42
celery
   gyoza 99
   pickled celery 136
chazuke 65–66
cheese, kushikatsu (fried skewers) 90
chicken
   chicken stock 27
   gyoza 99
   hiyashichuka (summer noodles) 41
   karaage (fried chicken) 75
   miso tsukemen (dipping noodles with miso) 34
   oyako don (rice with chicken & eggs) 53–54
   shio ramen 30
   shoyu ramen 29
   yakitori 107–08
chicken livers or heart, yakitori 107–08
coriander, tempura 87–88
cream, omuraisu (omelette & rice) 49–50
croquettes 83
cucumber
   hiyashichuka (summer noodles) 41
   pickled cucumber 135
   sushi 61

curry 10
   kare-raisu (Japanese curry) 127
dashi 19
   dashimaki tamago (Japanese omelette) 139
   dashi soup with eggs 128
   gomadare (sesame sauce) 15
   miso soup with fresh cabbage 128
   miso soup with potatoes & onions 12
   nuku soba (hot soba) 37
   nuku udon (hot udon) 37
   onkonomiyaki (hearty cabbage pancakes) 111–12
   oyako don (rice with chicken & eggs) 53–54
   shoyu ramen 29
donburi 53–54, 56

eggs
   dashimaki tamago (Japanese omelette) 139
   dashi soup with eggs 128
   dashi with eggs 128
   gyudon (rice with beef) 56
   hiyashichuka (summer noodles) 41
   miso tsukemen (dipping noodles with miso) 34
   nama tamago (raw) 23
   nuku soba (hot soba) 37
   nuku udon (hot udon) 37
   omuraisu (omelette & rice) 49–50
   onkonomiyaki (hearty cabbage pancakes) 111–12
   onsen tamago (hot-spring) 23
   oyako don (rice with chicken & eggs) 53–54
   shabu shabu (Japanese hot pot) 121
   shio ramen 30
   shoyu ramen 29
   sukiyaki (stew with meat & vegetables) 118
   yude tamago (boiled) 23
   zuke tamago (marinated) 23

fish
   sashimi 133
   shake ikura chazuke (rice in tea with salmon & salmon roe) 65
   sushi 61
   teriyaki salmon 102
   zuke chazuke (rice in tea with marinated fish) 66
frying tips 73, 95

gari 11
   gyudon (rice with beef) 56
   onkonomiyaki (hearty cabbage pancakes) 111
   sushi 61
ginger
   chicken stock 27
   deep fried aubergines 16
   gyudon (rice with beef) 56
   hiyayakko with sesame oil 143
   miso tsukemen (dipping noodles with miso) 34
   oyako don (rice with chicken & eggs) 53–54
   shogayaki (fried pork in ginger sauce) 96
   taberu rayu (chunky umami oil) 14
   zuke chazuke (rice in tea with marinated fish) 66
gochujang, miso tsukemen (dipping noodles with miso) 34
gomadare 15
goma dressing 15
green beans, otsumami (quick dishes) 16
gyoza 99
gyudon 56

ham, hiyashichuka (summer noodles) 41
Hiroshima yaki 112
hiyashichuka 41
hiyayakko, hiyayakko with katsuobushi 143

ice cream, pafe (parfait) 146
ichiban dashi 19
ichijuu sansai 148

Japanese curry 127
Japanese meals 148
Japanese omelette 139
Japanese stock 19

karaage 75
kare-raisu 127
katsuobushi 10
   hiyayakko with katsuobushi 143
   ichiban dashi (dashi with kombu & katsuobushi) 19
   miso tsukemen (dipping noodles with miso) 34
   okoka (fried katsuobushi) 20
   onkonomiyaki (hearty cabbage pancakes) 111–12
   taberu rayu (chunky umami oil) 14
   yakisoba 42
katsusando 81
ketchup
   bannou sauce 13
   omuraisu (omelette & rice) 49–50
   tonkatsu 78
kombu 10
   chicken stock 27
   ichiban dashi 19
   okobu (stewed kombu) 20
   ponzu (soy & citrus) 14
   shabu shabu (Japanese hot pot) 121
   sushi 61
   tare 13
korokke 83
kushikatsu 90

leeks, shabu shabu (Japanese hot pot) 121
lemon juice, ponzu (soy & citrus) 14
lettuce, shogayaki (fried pork in ginger sauce) 96
lime juice, ponzu (soy & citrus) 14
lunch boxes 144

matcha tea powder 10
   pafe (parfait) 146
mayonnaise 10
   katsusando 81
   onkonomiyaki (hearty cabbage pancakes) 111–12
   yakisoba 42
meals, ichijuu sansai 148
mirin 10
   gyudon (rice with beef) 56
   miso tsukemen (dipping noodles with miso) 34
   okobu (stewed kombu) 20
   okoka (fried katsuobushi) 20
   omuraisu (omelette & rice) 49–50
   oyako don (rice with chicken & eggs) 53–54
   tare 13
   zuke chazuke (rice in tea with marinated fish) 66
miso paste 10
   bannou sauce 13
   miso soup with fresh cabbage 128
   miso soup with potatoes & onions 128
   miso tsukemen 34
shogayaki (fried pork in ginger sauce) 96
taberu rayu (chunky umami oil) 14
tonkatsu 78
zuke chazuke (rice in tea with marinated fish) 66
mushrooms
   chicken stock 27
   kushikatsu (fried skewers) 90
   omuraisu (omelette & rice) 49–50
   otsumami (quick dishes) 16
   shabu shabu (Japanese hot pot) 121
   sukiyaki (stew with meat & vegetables) 118
   sushi 61
   taberu rayu (chunky umami oil) 14
   tempura 87–88
   yakitori 107–08
mustard 11
   hiyashichuka (summer noodles) 41
   katsusando 81

nama tamago 23
niban dashi 20
noodles 25
see also ramen

hiyashichuka (summer noodles)	41	
miso tsukemen	34	
nuku soba (hot soba)	37	
nuku udon (hot udon)	37	
sukiyaki (stew with meat & vegetables)	118	
yakisoba	42	
nori		10
hiyashichuka (summer noodles)	41	
miso tsukemen (dipping noodles with miso)	34	
onigiri	69	
shake ikura chazuke (rice in tea with salmon & salmon roe)	65	
sushi	61	
nuku soba	37	
nuku udon	37	
octopus, onkonomiyaki (hearty cabbage pancakes)	111–12	
okobu	20	
okoka	20	
omelettes		
dashimaki tamago (Japanese omelette)	139	
omuraisu (omelette & rice)	49–50	
omuraisu	49	
onigiri	69	
onions		
gyudon (rice with beef)	56	
kare-raisu (Japanese curry)	127	
korokke (croquettes)	83	
miso soup with potatoes & onions	128	
miso with potatoes & onions	128	
omuraisu (omelette & rice)	49–50	
otsumami (quick dishes)	16	
oyako don (rice with chicken & eggs)	53–54	
taberu rayu (chunky umami oil)	14	
yakisoba	42	
onkonomiyaki		
Hiroshima yaki	112	
Osaka-style	111	
onsen tamago	23	
otsumami	16	
oyako don	53–54	
pafe	146	
panko breadcrumbs		11
katsusando	81	
korokke (croquettes)	83	
kushikatsu (fried skewers)	90	
tonkatsu (panko-fried pork)	78	
parfait	146	
peppers, omuraisu (omelette & rice)	49–50	
pickles		
pickled carrot	136	
pickled celery	136	
pickled Chinese cabbage	136	
pickled cucumber	135	
pickled radish	135	
ponzu	14	
sashimi	133	
tomato quick dish	16	
pork		
gyoza	99	
onkonomiyaki (hearty cabbage pancakes)	111–12	
shogayaki (fried pork in ginger sauce)	96	
tonkatsu	78	
potatoes		
kare-raisu (Japanese curry)	127	
korokke (croquettes)	83	
miso soup with potatoes & onions	128	
prawns		
gyoza	99	
kushikatsu (fried skewers)	90	
onkonomiyaki (hearty cabbage pancakes)	111–12	
radish, pickled	135	
ramen		
shio ramen	30	
shoyu ramen	29	
rice		11, 45
batch cooking	7	
boiled rice	47	
gomadare (sesame sauce)	15	
gyudon (rice with beef)	56	
home-made sushi	61	
omuraisu (omelette & rice)	49–50	

onigiri (rice balls)	69	
oyako don (rice with chicken & eggs)	53–54	
shabu shabu (Japanese hot pot)	121	
shake ikura chazuke (rice in tea with salmon & salmon roe)	65	
sushi	61	
zuke chazuke (rice in tea with marinated fish)	66	
rice vinegar		10
goma dressing (sesame dressing)	15	
hiyashichuka (summer noodles)	41	
sushi	61	
tare (soy-based glaze)	13	
tsukemono (pickles)	135–36	
sake		10
gyudon (rice with beef)	56	
okobu (stewed kombu)	20	
omuraisu (omelette & rice)	49–50	
tare (soy-based glaze)	13	
salmon		
sashimi	133	
shake ikura chazuke (rice in tea with salmon & salmon roe)	65	
sushi	61	
teriyaki salmon	102	
zuke chazuke (rice in tea with marinated fish)	66	
salmon roe		
hiyayakko with salmon roe	143	
shake ikura chazuke (rice in tea with salmon & salmon roe)	65	
sashimi	133	
sauces		
bannou sauce	13	
ponzu (soy & citrus)	14	
taberu rayu (chunky umami oil)	14	
tare	13	
sesame oil		11
goma dressing (sesame dressing)	15	
hiyayakko with sesame oil	143	
taberu rayu (chunky umami oil)	14	
sesame paste		11
gomadare (sesame sauce)	15	
miso tsukemen	34	
sesame seeds		11
goma dressing (sesame dressing)	15	
taberu rayu (chunky umami oil)	14	
shabu shabu	121	
shake ikura chazuke	65	
shake teriyaki	102	
shichimi togarashi		
nuku soba (hot soba)	37	
nuku udon (hot udon)	37	
shio ramen	30	
shogayaki	96	
shoyu ramen	29	
soba, hot	37	
soup		
dashi with eggs	128	
miso with fresh cabbage	128	
miso with potatoes & onions	128	
soy sauce		11
bannou sauce	13	
gyudon (rice with beef)	56	
miso tsukemen (dipping noodles with miso)	34	
okobu (stewed kombu)	20	
okoka (fried katsuobushi)	20	
omuraisu (omelette & rice)	49–50	
oyako don (rice with chicken & eggs)	53–54	
ponzu (soy & citrus)	14	
sashimi	133	
shogayaki (fried pork in gingersauce)	96	
shoyu ramen	29	
sushi	61	
tonkatsu	78	
zuke chazuke (rice in tea with marinated fish)	66	
spinach, shabu shabu (Japanese hot pot)	121	
spring onions		
deep fried aubergines	16	
gyoza	99	
hiyashichuka (summer noodles)	41	
hiyayakko with sesame oil	143	
kushikatsu (fried skewers)	90	
miso tsukemen (dipping noodles with miso)	34	
nuku soba (hot soba)	37	

nuku udon (hot udon)	37	
onkonomiyaki (hearty cabbage pancakes)	111	
oyako don (rice with chicken & eggs)	53–54	
shabu shabu (Japanese hot pot)	121	
shake ikura chazuke (rice in tea with salmon & salmon roe)	65	
shio ramen	30	
shoyu ramen	29	
yakitori (chicken skewers)	107–08	
stock		
chicken stock	27	
Japanese stock	19	
strawberries, pafe (parfait)	146	
sugar		
bannou sauce	13	
gomadare (sesame sauce)	15	
gyudon (rice with beef)	56	
miso tsukemen (dipping noodles with miso)	34	
pafe (parfait)	146	
ponzu (soy & citrus)	14	
tare (soy-based glaze)	13	
sukiyaki	118	
sūpu	128	
sushi, home-made	61	
sweetcorn kakiage	87	
taberu rayu	14	
shio ramen	30	
shoyu ramen	29	
tahini		
gomadare (sesame sauce)	15	
miso tsukemen	34	
tare	13	
gyudon (rice with beef)	56	
hiyashichuka (summer noodles)	41	
teriyaki salmon	102	
zuke tamago (marinated eggs)	23	
tea		10
shake ikura chazuke (rice in tea with salmon & salmon roe)	65	
zuke chazuke (rice in tea with marinated fish)	66	
temakizushi	61	
tempura	87–88	
teriyaki salmon	102	
tofu		
hiyayakko with katsuobushi	143	
hiyayakko with salmon roe	143	
hiyayakko with sesame oil	143	
shabu shabu (Japanese hot pot)	121	
sukiyaki (stew with meat & vegetables)	118	
tomatoes		
hiyashichuka (summer noodles)	41	
otsumami (quick dishes)	16	
shogayaki (fried pork in ginger sauce)	96	
tonkatsu	78	
tsukemono	135–36	
udon		
nuku udon (hot udon)	37	
sukiyaki (stew with meat & vegetables)	118	
umami oil, chunky	14	
umeboshi		11
wakame		
nuku soba (hot soba)	37	
nuku udon (hot udon)	37	
walnuts, taberu rayu (chunky umami oil)	14	
wasabi		11
sashimi	133	
shake ikura chazuke (rice in tea with salmon & salmon roe)	65	
sushi	61	
wine, tare (soy-based glaze)	13	
Worcestershire sauce		
bannou sauce	13	
tonkatsu	78	
yakisoba	42	
yakitori	107–08	
yude tamago	23	
yuzu kosho		11
nuku soba (hot soba)	37	
nuku udon (hot udon)	37	
shio ramen	30	
zuke chazuke	66	
zuke tamago	23	

Thank you!

Thank you for the beautiful porcelain and ceramics:
Kinto Europe
Toshiaki Hoshi
Normal Object Factory
Ingrid Unsöld
Yoko Yamano

Many thanks to my amazing book team:
Photographer Ylva Sundgren
Designer Sebastian Wadsted
Editor Maria Nilsson
Thank you for the commitment and passion you have devoted to help me bring this project to life!

And Myo Ichihara, if you hadn't been born I would never have made a career change or thought about writing a book. I'm so proud to have done it. New challenges hold no fear when I think of you. I hope you will cook from this book when you're a little older. I love you to the moon and back.

DK LONDON
Editorial Director Cara Armstrong
Project Editor Izzy Holton
Senior Designer Tania Gomes
Sales and Jackets Coordinator Emily Cannings
DTP Coordinator Heather Blagden
Senior Production Editor Tony Phipps
Senior Production Controller Stephanie McConnell
Art Director Maxine Pedliham
Publishing Director Stephanie Jackson

DK DELHI
Pre-Production Coordinator Pushpak Tyagi
Pre-production Manager Balwant Singh

Editorial Sarah Epton
Translator Jane Davis

First published in Sweden by Natur & Kultur

First published in Great Britain in 2025 by
Dorling Kindersley Limited
20 Vauxhall Bridge Road,
London SW1V 2SA

The authorised representative in the EEA is
Dorling Kindersley Verlag GmbH. Arnulfstr. 124,
80636 Munich, Germany

Text copyright © Saori Ichihara and Natur & Kultur 2024
Design copyright © Sebastian Wadsted 2024
Photography copyright © Ylva Sundgren 2024
Copyright © 2025 Dorling Kindersley Limited
A Penguin Random House Company
10 9 8 7 6 5 4 3 2 1
001–352716–Oct/2025

All rights reserved.
No part of this publication may be reproduced, stored in or introduced into a retrieval system, or transmitted, in any form, or by any means (electronic, mechanical, photocopying, recording, or otherwise), without the prior written permission of the copyright owner.
DK values and supports copyright. Thank you for respecting intellectual property laws by not reproducing, scanning or distributing any part of this publication by any means without permission. By purchasing an authorised edition, you are supporting writers and artists and enabling DK to continue to publish books that inform and inspire readers.
No part of this publication may be used or reproduced in any manner for the purpose of training artificial intelligence technologies or systems. In accordance with Article 4(3) of the DSM Directive 2019/790, DK expressly reserves this work from the text and data mining exception.

A CIP catalogue record for this book
is available from the British Library.
ISBN: 978-0-2417-7246-1

Printed and bound in China

www.dk.com

This book was made with Forest Stewardship Council™ certified paper – one small step in DK's commitment to a sustainable future.
Learn more at www.dk.com/uk/information/sustainability